HARVARD STUDIES IN ADMINISTRATIVE LAW

VOLUME III

LONDON : HUMPHREY MILFORD
OXFORD UNIVERSITY PRESS

Administrative Tribunals and the Rules of Evidence

A STUDY IN JURISPRUDENCE
AND ADMINISTRATIVE LAW

BY

HAROLD M. STEPHENS

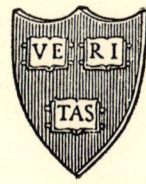

CAMBRIDGE
HARVARD UNIVERSITY PRESS
1933

COPYRIGHT, 1933
BY THE PRESIDENT AND FELLOWS OF HARVARD COLLEGE

353
S833a

JUN - 1 1933
320476
Max. Pol. Sci.

PRINTED AT THE HARVARD UNIVERSITY PRESS
CAMBRIDGE, MASS., U.S.A.

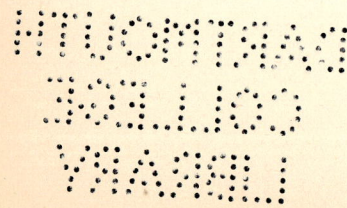

TO

MY FATHER AND MOTHER

PREFACE

THE wide field of activities committed to administrative tribunals, and the tendency to extend this field, together with the interesting attempts in many commissions to carry on their proceedings without the rules of evidence, warrant, it is believed, the present study, which covers the work of the Interstate Commerce Commission, the Federal Trade Commission, state public service commissions, hearings of tax assessment and equalization tribunals in the states, and the alien deportation and exclusion hearings of the United States Bureau of Immigration. It is hoped that the examination of statutes, rules of practice, judicial decisions, and of the actual practice in the commissions may be of some use to commissioners, lawyers who appear before commissions, judges who review commission orders, and teachers. Commissioners in one field, or in one state, may find it at least of interest to compare their methods and the reactions of the courts thereto with those in others; lawyers, judges, and teachers may find of use the collection into one place of the cases and other materials; all, it is hoped, will find of some value the summaries and comparisons, and the conclusions drawn from the data examined.

I express my appreciation to Dean Roscoe Pound and to Professor Felix Frankfurter for stimulating suggestions. I thank the many commissioners who generously took time to furnish the material for Chapter V.

H. M. S.

CAMBRIDGE, MASSACHUSETTS
January 1, 1933

CONTENTS

I. INTRODUCTION 3

II. LEGISLATION 7
    A. Interstate Commerce Commission 7
    B. Federal Trade Commission 8
    C. State Public Service Commissions 9
    D. United States Bureau of Immigration 15

III. RULES 16
    A. Interstate Commerce Commission 16
    B. Federal Trade Commission 16
    C. State Public Service Commissions 16
    D. United States Bureau of Immigration 18

IV. JUDICIAL DECISIONS 20
    A. Interstate Commerce Commission 20
    B. Federal Trade Commission 31
    C. State Public Service Commissions 32
    D. Taxation 46
    E. Alien Exclusion and Deportation Hearings 51
        1. Statement of General Rule 53
        2. Impeachment 55
        3. Conclusions 56
        4. Evidence Immaterial because not Connected 56
        5. Former Conviction 57
        6. Denial of Cross-Examination 57
        7. Testimony of Wife against Husband 58
        8. Unsworn Interpreters 59
        9. Hearsay 59
            (a) Miscellaneous Cases 59
            (b) Hearsay in the Form of Affidavits 64
            (c) Records in other Proceedings 64

V. THE PRACTICE IN THE COMMISSIONS: QUESTIONNAIRE 68

VI. SUMMARIES AND COMPARISONS 85
    A. Legislation 85
    B. Rules 86
    C. Judicial Decisions 86

    D. The Practice in the Commissions 87
    E. Comparison of the Courts' and Commissions' Reasons for not Applying the Rules of Evidence 89
    F. Comparison of the Judicial Decisions in each Class of Cases, in respect to the Rules of Evidence Infringed by the Commissions and Types of Matter Admitted 89

VII. CONCLUSIONS 92

APPENDICES
    I. PUBLIC SERVICE COMMISSION STATUTES CONTAINING NO PROVISION CONCERNING THE RULES OF EVIDENCE 107
    II. REFERENCES TO IMMIGRATION STATUTES EXAMINED 108
    III. REFERENCES TO RULES EXAMINED 110

TABLE OF AUTHORITIES 113

INDEX 121

ADMINISTRATIVE TRIBUNALS AND
THE RULES OF EVIDENCE

CHAPTER I

INTRODUCTION

THE rules of evidence have been thought to have value in seeking facts. Dean Wigmore,[1] discussing conflicting views as to the applicability of the rules of evidence to the hearings of administrative tribunals, well states the orthodox view of the lawyer and judge in saying: "The . . . technical view is that the jury-trial system of rules is the only safe method of investigation where liberty and property may be at stake; that the sound wisdom of caution which is the basis of that system is as valid for one tribunal as for another; and that the judicial review of administrative officers' findings would be impracticable and ineffective without using that system as a standard for checking the regularity of the proceedings. — There is no need to quote representatives of this view; it preaches or lurks in almost every judicial opinion; and it echoes instantly in the breast of the orthodox legal practitioner." To the contrary, and with at least equal vigor, the same author states:[2] " . . . The popular view, it may be called — is that the jury trial rules have had their day in our system of justice; that their obstructive and irrational technicalities have made the system nauseous and futile in its native habitat; and that to transplant it to new fields would be an error amounting to a folly. . . ." Writers on Administrative Law themselves suggest that this popular view is finding favor and currency in the practice of the tribunals: "Administrative tribunals are not bound by the procedural safeguards which mould the outcome of an action at law; more specifically, they are, in the first place, not bound by the common-law rules of evidence. . . ."[3] Again, in respect to the Federal Trade Commission:[4] "So far as I have been able to find, the commission itself has never refused to give effect to testimony on the ground that it is technically incompetent; nor have questions of the law of evidence played any part in the cases on appeal. As has

---

[1] 1 Wigmore, *Evidence* (2d ed. 1923), § 4b, p. 28.
[2] *Idem*, p. 27.
[3] Dickinson, *Administrative Justice and the Supremacy of Law* (1927), p. 35.
[4] Henderson, *Federal Trade Commission* (1924), p. 64.

been pointed out, the rules of evidence grew out of the practical exigencies of trial by jury and are probably superfluous in an administrative proceeding. . . ."[5]

But "Administrative Law is groping; it necessarily is still crudely empirical. It is dealing with new problems, calling for new social inventions or fresh adaptations of old experiences . . . ";[6] and in this state of the subject " . . . what jurist and judge and legislator must do for a season is to re-examine the rules and principles and doctrines, which were defined so sharply and worked out so thoroughly in all their logical implications in the last century and to reshape them to accord with the exigencies of this newly recognized social interest in the individual life."[7]

In such a state of the law, and under such prompting, it is warranted to study every phase of Administrative Law in actual operation. Investigation of the general subject of the applicability of the common-law rules of evidence to the proceedings of administrative tribunals was commenced by Mr. Frank A. Ross.[8] It is intended here to carry the investigation into the activities of the Interstate Commerce Commission, the Federal Trade Commission, the public service commissions of the several states, the hearings of tax assessment and equalization tribunals in the several states, and the alien deportation and exclusion hearings of the Bureau of Immigration, United States Department of Labor.

The subject is of interest from the standpoint of the science of law. It is important to both society and the individual that the orders of all tribunals have a foundation in fact. If the orthodox lawyers' view that only through the use of the rules of evidence can we dependably find the facts is correct, then following the popular view and abandoning the use of these safeguards to the truth is a perhaps greater individualization of the administration of justice than even the most spirited protagonists of commissions would endorse. For already the administrative official has been freed from the restraints of the more rigid rules of substantive law

[5] And see Freund, *Administrative Powers over Persons and Property* (1928), p. 169, § 83.

[6] Frankfurter and Davison, *Cases on Administrative Law* (1932), Preface, p. vii.

[7] Pound, *The Revival of Personal Government*, New Hampshire Bar Association Proceedings (1917), 13, 33; Pound, *The Administrative Application of Legal Standards*, XLIV *A.B.A. Rep.* (1919), p. 445.

[8] Ross, *Applicability of Common Law Rules of Evidence in Proceedings before Workmen's Compensation Commissions* (1923), 36 Harv. L. Rev. 263.

and left much to his own discretion in the application of wide standards of reasonableness and adequacy and fairness. But now he is, by the relaxation or abandonment of the rules of evidence, to be "heart whole and fancy free" as to the facts. The "hunch" as the basis of decision will indeed have been canonized. But if the popular view is correct and the rules of evidence are but "obstructive and irrational technicalities," then we are well rid of them. Perhaps the truth lies part way between.

The materials covered by this study are the statutes governing the conduct of hearings in the several types of tribunals mentioned, the rules adopted by the commissions, the actual practice in the commissions as disclosed by the answers to a questionnaire sent to the chairmen of the Interstate Commerce Commission and the Federal Trade Commission, to the Commissioner General of Immigration, and to the chairman of each of the state public service commissions, and the judicial decisions in appellate courts in all cases in which error has been predicated upon the admission of evidence in violation of the common-law rules. The aim is to discover what rules of evidence are not applied, why they are not applied and, so far as possible, with what effect. To this end it has been thought necessary to set out herein, at some length, a statement or abstract of each case studied,[9] so that the data within which comparisons may be made, and from which conclusions may be drawn, may be before the reader.

Within the field thus limited to the study of the non-application of the rules of evidence in administrative hearings, the material has been still further restricted so as to include, except by incidental reference, only those rules of evidence which courts have thought of use, if not necessary, in obtaining accurate and honest evidence. That is to say, there are excluded from consideration such so-called rules of evidence as determine the burden of proof, and the duty of going forward with evidence, and presumptions, and rules having to do with the extent to which proof must be carried in respect to making it convincing, i.e., rules requiring proof by a preponderance of the evidence, or by clear and convincing testimony, or beyond a reasonable doubt, and rules determining what constitutes a prima facie case. In short, it is not intended to discuss cases having to do with rules of evidence, so called, which relate to the quantum or to the source, or to the duty of first pro-

[9] Where there are several cases of a type, but one will be stated in detail; the others will be referred to in footnotes.

ducing evidence. These rules are more procedural than strictly evidential in character; they have not to do with matters of dependability of evidence.

It is hoped that some light may be shed through a study of the data herein upon the question whether dependability is being sacrificed, and whether such sacrifice, if any, is necessary and justifiable.[10]

[10] This study has been limited to statutes in effect, rules adopted, and cases decided prior to January 1, 1932.

CHAPTER II

LEGISLATION

A. *Interstate Commerce Commission.* The United States statutes creating the Interstate Commerce Commission and defining and authorizing its activities are broadly phrased with reference to the scope and variety of its inquiries, and the machinery for and the manner of carrying them on. The Commission is given "authority to inquire into the management of the business of all common carriers subject to the provisions"[1] of the Act, and is authorized "to obtain from such common carriers full and complete information necessary to enable the Commission to perform the duties and carry out the objects for which it was created."[2] The Commission is empowered "to require, by subpoena, the attendance and testimony of witnesses and the production of all books, papers, tariffs, contracts, agreements, and documents relating to any matter under investigation."[3] It may require the "attendance of witnesses, and the production of . . . documentary evidence . . . from any place in the United States, at any designated place of hearing."[4] "It may, by one or more of the Commissioners, prosecute any inquiry necessary to its duties, in any part of the United States, into any matter or question of fact pertaining to the business of any common carrier subject to the provisions"[5] of the Act. "The testimony of any witness may be taken . . . in any proceeding or investigation pending before the Commission, by deposition. . . ."[6]

It was apparently the purpose of Congress to leave the Commission quite free with reference to the rules of evidence. The statutes do not say that the rules of evidence are applicable and do not, as do many of the state statutes in respect of state public service commissions, in terms provide that they are not applicable. That the trustworthiness of evidence is to be sanctioned by the taking

[1] 24 Stat. 383 (1887), 49 U. S. C., § 12 (1) (1926).   [2] *Ibid.*
[3] 25 Stat. 858, 859 (1889), 49 U. S. C., § 12 (1) (1926).
[4] 26 Stat. 743 (1891), 49 U. S. C., § 12 (2) (1926).
[5] 24 Stat. 386 (1887), 49 U. S. C., § 19 (2) (1926).
[6] 26 Stat. 743, 744 (1891), 49 U. S. C., § 12 (4) (1926).

of an oath or making of an affirmation is indicated. "Any member of the commission may administer oaths and affirmations. . . ."[7] The Commission is authorized to employ special agents or examiners who shall have power to administer oaths, examine witnesses, and receive evidence."[8] Every person deposing "shall be cautioned and sworn (or affirm, if he so request) to testify the whole truth, and shall be carefully examined. His testimony shall be reduced to writing . . . and . . . subscribed by the deponent."[9]

The manner of holding hearings and of taking evidence is prescribed in very general terms, resulting in wide powers to the Commission. Thus where a complaint is made of violation of law by a carrier ". . . it shall be the duty of the Commission to investigate the matters complained of in such manner and by such means as it shall deem proper [10] . . . and the said commission shall have the same powers and authority to proceed with any inquiry instituted on its own motion. . . ."[11] "The commission may conduct its proceedings in such manner as will best conduce to the proper dispatch of business and to the ends of justice. . . . The commission may, from time to time, make or amend such general rules or orders as may be requisite for the order and regulation of proceedings before it, or before any division of the commission. . . ."[12] In valuing the property of carriers ". . . except as herein otherwise provided, the commission shall have power to prescribe the method of procedure to be followed in the conduct of the investigation, the form in which the results of the valuation shall be submitted. . . ."[13]

B. *Federal Trade Commission.* The Federal Trade Commission Act [14] is silent as to the rules of evidence. Section 9 touching the power of the Commission to subpoena the attendance of witnesses, and the production of documentary evidence, and the taking of depositions, and the subject of incrimination and immunity, makes no provision at all concerning what kind of evidence the Commis-

[7] 40 Stat. 270 (1917), 49 U. S. C., § 17 (1) (1926).
[8] 34 Stat. 594, 595 (1906), 49 U. S. C., § 20 (10) (1926).
[9] 26 Stat. 743, 744 (1891), 49 U. S. C., § 12 (5) (1926).
[10] 24 Stat. 383, 384 (1887), 49 U. S. C., § 13 (1) (1926).
[11] 36 Stat. 550 (1910), 49 U. S. C., § 13 (2) (1926).
[12] 24 Stat. 385 (1887), 49 U. S. C., § 17 (1) (1926); 40 Stat. 270 (1917), 49 U. S. C., § 17 (1) (1926).
[13] 37 Stat. 701 (1913), 49 U. S. C., § 19a (c) (1926).
[14] 38 Stat. 717–724 (1914), 15 U. S. C., §§ 41–51 (1926).

sion may receive, or what, or how, rules of evidence shall be applied in hearings.

C. *State Public Service Commissions.*[15] Public service commission statutes are of several types so far as provisions are concerned which, either expressly, or by implication, relate to the rules of evidence.

1. Statutes authorizing the commissions to adopt reasonable and proper rules to govern their proceedings, and to regulate the mode and manner of hearings. In this category is the District of Columbia,[16] providing in terms as follows: " . . . The commission shall have power . . . to adopt and publish reasonable and proper rules to govern its proceedings and to regulate the mode and manner of all investigations and hearings of public utilities and other parties before it." To substantially the same effect, and in almost identical terms, are the statutes of Kansas,[17] Michigan,[18] Montana,[19] Nebraska,[20] Ohio,[21] Oregon,[22] Pennsylvania, whose statutes provide in even more simple terms,[23] " . . . and all hearings, investigations, and proceedings by the commission shall be governed by such rules, not inconsistent with this act, as shall be adopted and prescribed by the commission . . ."; Tennessee,[24] Texas,[25] Vermont,[26] Wyoming,[27] South Dakota,[28] where it is similarly pro-

[15] For convenience the state commissions empowered to regulate carriers and public service companies are, when referred to generally herein, called "public service commissions." The actual names vary with the states: In California such a commission is called the "Railroad Commission," in Colorado the "Public Utilities Commission," in Minnesota the "Railroad and Warehouse Commission," in North Carolina the "Corporation Commission," in Missouri the "Public Service Commission," etc.

In addition to the state statutes those of the District of Columbia and the territories of Alaska and Hawaii were also examined and are, for convenience, discussed with the state statutes.

[16] D. C. Code (1929), tit. 26, § 54.
[17] Kansas Rev. Stat. Ann. (1923), c. 66, § 106.
[18] Mich. Comp. Laws (1929), § 11018.
[19] Mont. Rev. Codes (Choate, 1921), § 3894.
[20] Neb. Comp. Stat. (1929), c. 75, § 301.
[21] Ohio Gen. Code (Page, 1932), § 499–6.
[22] Oregon Code Ann. (1930), § 61–110.
[23] Pa. Stat. Ann. (Purdon, 1930), tit. 66, § 711.
[24] Tenn. Code (1932), § 5399.
[25] Texas Rev. Civ. Code (Vernon, 1928), art. 6450.
[26] Vt. Gen. Laws (1917), § 5036.
[27] Wyoming Rev. Stat. (Courtright, 1931), § 94–150.
[28] S. D. Comp. Laws (1929), § 9497.

vided that the " . . . board may from time to time make or amend such general rules or orders as may be requisite for the order and regulation of proceedings before it . . . including forms and notices and the service thereof, which shall conform as nearly as may be to those in use in courts of this state. . . ." The Nevada statute [29] is in a similar category, though it somewhat more briefly states that " . . . The commission shall have the power to adopt and publish rules for the orderly conduct of proceedings before it." In New Mexico [30] it is provided that " . . . The commission and the supreme court are hereby authorized and empowered to make and publish further rules of order, practice and procedure as the commission or supreme court may deem necessary or proper."

2. Statutes like those just described [31] but providing also: "A substantial compliance by the commission with the requirements of this article shall be sufficient to give effect to all rules, orders, acts and regulations of the commission and they shall not be declared inoperative, illegal or void for any omission of a technical nature, in respect thereto." Such is the Alabama statute [32] and, in almost identical terms, the Wisconsin [33] statute.

3. A third class of statutes, in addition to authorizing the commissions to prescribe rules of practice and procedure, expressly relieves them of the duty of applying "the technical rules of evidence," and some of the legislatures in passing such acts, in extra zeal to unfetter the commissions, have added that "no informality" in taking testimony shall invalidate an order, or that the commission may "exercise its discretion" with a view to "doing justice." Thus, in Arizona [34] it is provided that " . . . All hearings and investigations before the commission or any commissioner shall be governed by this article, and by rules of practice and procedure to be adopted by the commission. Neither the commission nor any commissioner shall be bound by the technical rules of evidence, and no informality in any proceeding, or in the manner of taking testimony, before the commission or any commissioner shall invalidate any order, decision, rule or regulation made, approved or

[29] Nev. Comp. Laws (Hillyer, 1929), § 6105.
[30] N. M. Stat. Ann. (Courtright, 1929), § 134–1120.
[31] Under II C 1 *supra*.
[32] Ala. Code (Michie, 1928), §§ 9621, 9802, 9667.
[33] Wis. Stat. (1931), § 195.03 (1) (5).
[34] Ariz. Code (Struckmeyer, 1928), § 709.

CHAP. II]   THE RULES OF EVIDENCE   11

confirmed by the commission." In Arkansas [35] the legislature has prescribed that " . . . The Commission shall prescribe the rules of procedure and for taking of evidence in all matters that may come before it. In the investigation, preparation and hearings of cases, the Commission may not be bound by the strict technical rules of pleading and evidence, but in that behalf it may exercise such discretion as will facilitate their (its) efforts to understand and learn all the facts bearing upon the right and justice of the matters before (it) them." The California act [36] parallels Arizona in meaning, though its phrasing is not identical: " . . . All hearings, investigations and proceedings shall be governed by this act and by rules of practice and procedure to be adopted by the commission, and in the conduct thereof the technical rules of evidence need not be applied. No informality in any hearing, investigation or proceeding or in the manner of taking testimony shall invalidate any order, decision, rule or regulation made, approved or confirmed by the commission." In Colorado [37] the statute is like that in Arizona. In Hawaii [38] " . . . The commission may make and amend rules not inconsistent with law respecting the procedure before it, and shall not be bound by the strict rules of the common law relating to the admission or rejection of evidence, but may exercise its own discretion in such matters with a view to doing substantial justice." In Idaho [39] the hearings of the commission are governed by the statute and by "rules of practice and procedure to be adopted by the commission, and in the conduct thereof neither the commission nor any commissioner shall be bound by the technical rules of evidence." The Illinois law gives the Commerce Commission " . . . power to adopt . . . proper rules to govern its proceedings, and to regulate the mode and manner of all investigations and hearings . . .,"[40] and then in substantially the terms of the Arizona act relieves the Commission from the "technical rules of evidence" and from invalidation of its action by reason of "informality."[41] The Maryland act [42] is like that of Idaho. In

[35] Ark. Dig. Stat. (Crawford and Moses, 1921), § 1683.
[36] Cal. Gen. Laws (Deering, 1923), Act 6386, § 53.
[37] Col. Ann. Stat. (Mills, 1930), § 5933L.
[38] Hawaii Rev. Laws (1925), § 2200.
[39] Idaho Comp. Stat. (1919), § 2478.
[40] Ill. Rev. Stat. (Cahill, 1931), c. 111a, § 23.
[41] *Idem*, § 79.
[42] Md. Ann. Code (Bagby, 1924), art. 23, § 358.

Missouri [43] the law follows in substance the Arizona provision. The New Hampshire statute,[44] the New Jersey law [45] and the New York act [46] are in substance the same as the Maryland and Idaho statutes. In North Dakota [47] the provision, otherwise similar to those in the Arizona and California statutes, specifically forbids the commission to apply the rules of evidence, stating " . . . All hearings shall be governed by this act and by the rules and practice and procedure to be adopted by the commissioners and in the conduct thereof the technical rules of evidence shall not be applied. No informality . . . etc." The Rhode Island law [48] is similar to the Idaho statute, except that it does not expressly provide that the hearings before the commission shall be governed by the statute as well as by the rules of practice to be adopted by the commission. The Utah statute [49] follows the California act in almost identical words. West Virginia [50] follows Arkansas, except that in the latter state the commission in its hearings " . . . may not be bound by the strict technical rules of pleading and evidence . . .," whereas in the former " . . . The commission shall not be bound by the technical rules of pleading and evidence. . . ."

4. Nothing but "expediency," "relevancy," "the proper dispatch of business," or "the ends of justice" is to limit the commissions of four states in the conduct of their hearings. Thus in Iowa [51] " . . . The board may in all cases conduct its proceedings, when not otherwise prescribed by law, in such manner as will best conduce to the proper dispatch of business and the attainment of justice." The Minnesota legislature,[52] in addition to authorizing the commission to make rules and orders requisite for the order and regulation of proceedings before it, " . . . including forms of notices and service thereof, which shall conform as nearly as may be to those in use in the courts . . .," has provided that the commission " . . . shall conduct its proceedings in such a manner as

[43] Mo. Rev. Stat. (1929), § 5144.
[44] N. H. Pub. Laws (1926), c. 238, §§ 9 and 10.
[45] N. J. Comp. Stat. (Supp. 1924), p. 2893, § 167–46.
[46] N. Y. Cons. Laws (Cahill, 1930) c. 49, § 20 — N. Y. Pub. Serv. Comm. Law (1910).
[47] N. D. Comp. Laws Ann. (Supp. 1925), § 4609c24.
[48] R. I. Gen. Laws (1923) c. 253, § 17.
[49] Utah Comp. Laws (1917), § 4820.
[50] W. Va. Code (1931) c. 24, art. I, § 7.
[51] Iowa Code (1931), § 7867.
[52] Minn. Stat. (Mason, 1927), § 4636.

will best conduce to the proper dispatch of business and to the ends of justice." In Kentucky,[53] "Said commission . . . shall hear such statements, arguments or evidence offered by the parties as the commission may deem relevant. . . ." In Oklahoma the statute [54] investing the Corporation Commission with jurisdiction to determine whether or not there exists a public necessity, and whether public convenience requires construction or operation of public telephone lines or exchanges, provides: " . . . Upon the hearing of such petition (for a certificate of convenience and necessity) any person interested may appear and file objections thereto and offer evidence in support thereof. And the Commission may summon such other witnesses and require the production of such other evidence as it may deem expedient, and shall have and possess all powers incident and necessary to a full and complete investigation of such petition, and the objections thereto. . . ." In respect to hearings on applications for similar certificates for power and heat, light, gas, electricity, or water utility construction, the Oklahoma Commission may require " . . . the production of such other evidence as it may deem proper." [55]

5. Certain of the state commissions are required to apply the rules of evidence. Thus the Florida statute [56] provides: " . . . In all cases under the provisions of this Chapter the rules of evidence shall be the same as in civil actions, except as hereinbefore otherwise provided." [57] There is a similar provision in Georgia,[58] with a similar unimportant exception clause.[59] In Maine,[60] with respect to rulings on evidence by an examiner appointed by the commission, it is provided: "When objection is made to the admissibility of evidence the examiner shall note the same with the reasons therefor and incorporate such notation and reasons in his report of the evidence according to the practice in taking depositions. The commission shall disregard or consider the evidence so objected to according to the rules governing the taking of evidence before the commission, and shall report its rulings thereon in its decision of

[53] Ky. Stat. (Carroll, 1930), § 201e–14, § 201e–22.
[54] Okla. Comp. Stat. Ann. (Bunn, 1921), §§ 3487, 3488.
[55] Comp. Okla. Stat. Ann. (Supp. Thornton, 1926), §§ 5459–5, 5459–6.
[56] Fla. Comp. Laws (1927), § 6738.
[57] The subjects of the exception do not relate to such rules of evidence as are germane to this study. *Idem*, §§ 6721 and 6731 (par. 4).
[58] Ga. Code Ann. (Michie, 1926), § 2641.
[59] *Idem*, §§ 2626, 2636, 2637.
[60] Me. Rev. Stat. (1930) c. 62, § 59.

the case"; and the statute then further provides:[61] " . . . In all actions and proceedings arising under this chapter all processes shall be served and the practice and rules of evidence shall be the same as in civil actions in the superior court except as otherwise herein provided."[62] The North Carolina statute is worded similarly to the Florida and Georgia acts.[63] As will be noted later, these provisions requiring application of the rules of evidence as in courts are not always obeyed.

6. There is a unique statute in Virginia.[64] It reads: "Proceedings to be as in courts of record — The commission, on hearing of all complaints, proceedings, contests, or controversies, in which it shall be called upon to decide or render judgment in its capacity as a court of record, shall observe and administer the common and statute law rules of evidence as observed and administered by the courts of this Commonwealth in like manner as complainants and defendants in the courts of this Commonwealth." The statute lacks clarity as to when the commission is to act as a court of record and as to whether, if under some circumstances it does not act as a court of record, the rules of evidence are then to be applied.[65]

7. In Delaware there is no public service commission, and there is none in Alaska. In Connecticut, Indiana, Louisiana, Massachusetts, Mississippi, South Carolina, and Washington there are commissions, but the statutes governing their proceedings have no provisions which either expressly or by implication relate to the application of the rules of evidence by the commissions themselves.[66]

[61] Me. Rev. Stat. (1930), c. 62, § 67.

[62] The exception here apparently refers to § 66 concerning burden of proof, and § 68 concerning self-incrimination, in the same chapter.

[63] N. C. Code Ann. (Michie, 1931), § 1093.

[64] Va. Code Ann. (Michie, 1930), § 3723.

[65] In the only decision found on the question of evidence in commission hearings the Supreme Court of Virginia held — (the case was decided under a previous statute similarly worded — Clause 23, § 1313a, Code of 1904, Acts 1902–03–04, pp. 137, 143) — in an appeal from a hearing before the commission to inquire into the necessity of a grade crossing by one railroad over the right of way of another, that it was erroneous for the commission itself to call and hear witnesses, one of whom was not sworn, and who were not called by the litigants, but that the error was harmless because of other evidence in the case sufficient to support the commission's finding. Norfolk and W. R. Co. *v.* Tidewater R. Co., 105 Va. 129, 52 S. E. 852 (1906).

[66] References to the statutes covering public service commissions in the seven states last mentioned are set forth in Appendix I.

D. *United States Bureau of Immigration.* A search of the United States statutes relating to immigration discloses no provisions with respect to the application of the rules of evidence in deportation and exclusion hearings.[67]

[67] There appears in Appendix II a list of references to the statutes examined.

CHAPTER III

RULES

A. *Interstate Commerce Commission.* The rules of practice adopted by the Interstate Commerce Commission contain nothing of importance in respect to the application of the rules of evidence in the Commission's hearings. It is apparently intended that the exhibits offered shall be subjected to some scrutiny as to their trustworthiness, and that only material and relevant evidence shall be considered.[1]

B. *Federal Trade Commission.* There is no provision in the rules of practice of the Federal Trade Commission as to the applicability of the rules of evidence. Rule IX provides that objections to evidence shall be in short form, stating the grounds of objections relied on. Rule XIII provides for the taking of depositions. Rule XIV has to do with the elimination of irrelevant and immaterial matter from documentary evidence by the filing of copies of the relevant and material matter only. These are the only provisions concerning evidence.[2]

C. *State Public Service Commissions.*[3] Of the rules examined,

[1] Rule XIII (a), (b), (c), (g) and (h), Rules of Practice as revised and amended to March 15, 1930, Vol. 4, Interstate Commerce Acts Ann., pp. 3437 to 3505 inclusive.

[2] Rules of Practice of the Federal Trade Commission, 1913. See Annual Report, Federal Trade Commission, for the fiscal year ended June 30, 1931, pp. 148 to 151 inclusive.

[3] The rules of practice of the following commissions were examined: Alabama, Arkansas, Arizona, California, Colorado, District of Columbia, Territory of Hawaii, Idaho, Illinois, Iowa, Kentucky, Louisiana, Maine, Maryland, Michigan, Missouri, Nebraska, Nevada, New Hampshire, New Jersey, New Mexico, New York, North Carolina, Ohio, Oklahoma, Oregon, Pennsylvania, Rhode Island, Porto Rico, South Carolina, Tennessee, Texas, Utah, Virginia, Washington, West Virginia, and Wisconsin.

Rules were not available for the states of Connecticut, Florida, Georgia, Kansas, Mississippi, Montana, North Dakota, South Dakota, Vermont, and Wyoming.

Delaware has no commission. Massachusetts has no formulated rules (C. C. H. P. U. and Carriers Service [1930], p. 1503). Minnesota has adopted no rules. Indiana revoked its rules in 1929 (C. C. H. P. U. and Carriers Service [1930], p. 1505).

few have provisions pertinent to this study. In the District of Columbia [4] a complete revision of the 1927 Rules of Procedure was made as of August 1929. It contained the following provision: [5] "The receipt of hearsay or secondary evidence by the Commission without objection or over objection shall not affect the weight to be accorded such evidence." The revision referred to was never formally adopted, but according to the chairman of the Commission "the Commission's practice has been substantially in accord therewith." [6] There were adopted by this Commission "Rules for Conduct of Hearing in Case No. 205" [7] containing in paragraph 8 thereof a provision identical with that quoted above. It is not clear why the Commission should see fit thus to bind itself in advance to give face value to all hearsay or secondary evidence. The provision is unique.

In Illinois, consistently with the statute referred to herein [8] authorizing the commission to adopt reasonable and proper rules to govern its proceedings and the mode and manner of investigations and hearings, the commission has adopted the following rule: "In the conduct of any investigation, inquiry or hearing, neither the Commission nor any Commissioner or officer of the Commission shall be bound by the technical rules of evidence, and no informality in any proceeding or in the manner of taking testimony . . . shall invalidate any . . . decision . . . made . . . by the Commission." [9] In Iowa, where the statute as set forth herein [10] broadly provides that the board may in all cases conduct its proceedings, when not otherwise prescribed by law, in such manner as will best conduce to the proper dispatch of business and the attainment of justice, the rules provide: " . . . Each party to the hearing will be allowed to introduce such evidence as is admis-

In Appendix III will be found references to the rules examined. An attempt was made to examine the rules of the commission for each state, territory (and the District of Columbia) in which rules are in force. A letter requesting a copy of its rules was sent to each commission, and all available material in the Harvard Law School Library was searched, including the P. U. and Carriers Service of the Commerce Clearing House.

[4] Again discussed, for convenience, with the state commission rules.
[5] Rule XI (h).
[6] Quoted from a letter in response to the questionnaire.
[7] An important rate case.
[8] II C *supra*.
[9] Rule 7, Rules of Practice and Procedure, C. C. H. P. U. and Carriers Service (1930), p. 607.
[10] II C *supra*.

sible under the general rules of evidence in the district courts of the State of Iowa and such other evidence as in the judgment of the Commission [sic] may be pertinent, material and admissible. . . ."[11] That is to say, the board binds itself to admit what a court would admit, but leaves itself free to admit what a court would not.

In Maine, the commission has provided by rule: "In all actions and proceedings [12] the practices and rules of evidence shall be the same as in civil actions in the Supreme Judicial Court, except as otherwise provided in said chapter."[13]

In New Mexico, where the statute [14] provides that the commission and the supreme court are authorized to make further rules of order, practice and procedure as the commission or supreme court may deem necessary or proper, the commission has adopted the rule that " . . . the Commission will at every stage of the proceeding, disregard any error or defect in the pleadings or proceedings which shall not affect the substantial rights of the parties. . . ."[15]

In Washington, where there is no statutory provision concerning the rules of evidence, the matter of their application is left to the good taste of the commissioners under a rule providing that "rules of evidence and procedure obtaining in court procedure will be followed in so far as they are appropriate."[16]

D. *United States Bureau of Immigration.* Except for requirements generally indicating that it is the intention of the Bureau that its orders shall be predicated upon facts elicited at hearings and that evidence shall be "relevant and material" the Immigration Rules [17] contain nothing concerning the application of the rules of evidence. It is provided [18] in respect to arrest and depor-

---

[11] Rule XI (b), Report of the Board of Railroad Commissioners (1912), p. 225. [12] Under the chapter.

[13] Rule IX, Rules of Practice and Procedure, Public Utilities Commission of Maine, 1926. This is in substance the wording of the Maine statute described in II C *supra*, except that the statute uses the words "Superior Court" instead of the words "Supreme Judicial Court." The statute is later than the rule, being a part of the Revision of 1930.

[14] As stated in II C *supra*.

[15] Rule II, Additional Rules of Procedure of State Corporation Commission, 1913. But this commission in practice applies the rules of evidence. See V *infra*.

[16] Rule XI, Practice and Procedure before Department of Public Works of Washington, 1929.

[17] Immigration Laws and Rules of January 1, 1930, United States Government Printing Office. [18] Rule 19, D, 1.

CHAP. III]   THE RULES OF EVIDENCE   19

tation on warrant [19] that " . . . the alien shall . . . be granted a hearing [20] to enable him to show cause, if any there be, why he should not be deported. . . ." It is required [21] that "boards of special inquiry [22] shall determine all cases as promptly as circumstances permit, due regard being had to the necessity of giving the alien a fair hearing. . . ." In respect to the imposition of fines upon transportation companies for bringing to the United States aliens afflicted with certain named diseases detectable by medical examination at the time of embarkation,[23] it is provided that the boards of special inquiry " . . . shall be careful to develop in the course of their hearings all facts and circumstances material to a determination of the transportation company's liability to such fine."[24] "Where the certificate of the medical examiner [25] fails to particularly describe the nature, character, and extent of the physical defect which it is certified may affect the ability of the alien to earn a living, boards of special inquiry shall call such examiner as a witness and interrogate him fully as to the particular nature, character, and extent of the affliction certified. Such testimony shall be made a part of the record."

Witnesses and papers and documents may be subpoenaed, but " . . . the power to issue subpoenas should be exercised only when absolutely necessary . . .," and if the witness is to be subpoenaed for the alien the latter " . . . shall be required . . . to show affirmatively that the proposed evidence is relevant and material. . . ."[26]

[19] The deportation procedure is explained in IV E *infra*.
[20] Before the person or persons named in the warrant of arrest.
[21] Rule 12, B, 1.
[22] See IV E *infra* for a description of such boards.
[23] Rule 23.
[24] Rule 12, C, 1.
[25] Rule 12, C, 2. This rule, it seems, would make admissible in evidence a medical certificate.
[26] Rule 24, A, 1.

CHAPTER IV

JUDICIAL DECISIONS

A. *Interstate Commerce Commission.* The position of the courts toward the refusals or omissions of the Interstate Commerce Commission to apply the rules of evidence has been developed and stated in eight cases in United States courts, to be discussed in the order of their dates. The utterance of the first upon the subject, *Interstate Commerce Commission* v. *Baird*,[1] is a dictum, but it is so widely quoted by both federal and state courts as the source of and authority for the rule, that it has attained in effect the dignity of a holding. The case involved an inquiry into railroad rates for coal transportation from Pennsylvania to the Atlantic seaboard. The rates were alleged to discriminate in favor of producing mining companies through the device of creation by the railroads of subsidiary, stock-controlled, coal-purchasing companies which, it was asserted, made total-output purchase contracts with the producing companies, thereby acted as shippers of the coal to the seaboard, and sold the same to customers to whom the producing mines, themselves, would otherwise directly have made sale. The subsidiaries, it was charged, paid such a price to the coal-producing companies as the latter would actually have received had they been the shippers and the rate to them fixed at a point below the usual charge to competing mines. During the hearing before the Interstate Commerce Commission, officers of the railroads, who were also officers of the subsidiary companies, were asked by the Commission to submit the purchase contracts, and to answer orally questions concerning them. They refused, upon the ground that the contracts and the questions related to the purchase and sale of coal, not to shipping rates, and to intrastate transactions, and were therefore not within the issues or within the jurisdiction of the Commission. The Commission petitioned the Circuit Court of the United States for the Southern District of New York for an order requiring the production of the contracts and requiring the witnesses to answer. The petition was denied. Upon appeal to the

[1] 194 U. S. 25 (1904).

THE RULES OF EVIDENCE

Supreme Court, it was held, the court speaking through Mr. Justice Day,[2] that the question was one of relevancy of proof which " . . . does not depend upon the conclusiveness of the testimony offered, but upon its legitimate tendency to establish a controverted fact. Relevancy is that 'quality of evidence which renders it properly applicable in determining the truth or falsity of the matter in issue between the parties to a suit.'";[3] and the court held that the contracts and testimony here sought were relevant, and should have been produced, and that the lower court erred in refusing so to order. The court then said: "The inquiry of a board of the character of the Interstate Commerce Commission should not be too narrowly constrained by technical rules as to the admissibility of proof. Its function is largely one of investigation and it should not be hampered in making inquiry pertaining to interstate commerce by those narrow rules which prevail in trials at common law where a strict correspondence is required between allegation and proof."[4] This is the dictum. The case holds merely that evidence, relevant to the issues within the test above stated, is admissible and must be produced upon demand. But, through the dictum, the case is a source of the widely quoted and generally followed rule in federal and state courts respecting not relevancy, but competency, that administrative tribunals are not bound by the rules of evidence.

In the next case to arise, *Interstate Commerce Commission* v. *Louisville & N. R. Co.*,[5] a carrier, after notification by the Interstate Commerce Commission that through rates must not exceed the sum of locals, from New Orleans to Mobile and from Mobile to Montgomery, raised the locals. At the instance of the New Orleans Board of Trade, the Commission upon a hearing set aside, as unfair, the local rates thus established, and directed the carrier to restore the old locals and make corresponding reductions in the through rates. The carrier, failing in the Circuit Court of the United States for Kentucky to obtain a temporary injunction against the Commission's order, upon a transfer of the suit to the Commerce Court prevailed, under a holding that the order of the Commission was void for lack of material evidence to support it. Upon appeal to the Supreme Court from a decree annulling the order the government asserted that, since the statute required the

[2] 194 U. S. 25, 44 (1904).
[3] Citing 1 (correctly II) Bouvier, Law Dictionary, Rawle's Revision (1897), 866. [4] 194 U. S. 25, 44 (1904). [5] 227 U. S. 88 (1912).

Commission to obtain information necessary to perform its duties and gave it legislative powers to make rates, it could act as Congress would, on its own information, and that, therefore, its findings must be presumed to have been supported thereby, even though its information was not formally proved at the hearing. The Supreme Court, speaking through Mr. Justice Lamar,[6] held otherwise, saying: "The Commission is an administrative body and, even where it acts in a quasi-judicial capacity, is not limited by the strict rules, as to the admissibility of evidence, which prevail in suits between private parties. . . ."[7] But the more liberal the practice in admitting testimony, the more imperative the obligation to preserve the essential rules of evidence by which rights are asserted or defended. In such cases the Commissioners cannot act upon their own information as could jurors in primitive days."[8]

Spiller v. *Atchison, Topeka & Santa Fe Ry.*[9] arose next in point of time and is the first case directly considering evidence not ordinarily received in a court of law. The case was an action in the District Court of the United States for Missouri by the plaintiff, as assignee of the claims of a large number of shippers of cattle, against nine different railroad companies for the recovery of reparations awarded against them respectively by the Interstate Commerce Commission. There was a judgment for the plaintiff, a reversal thereof in the Circuit Court of Appeals, and a reversal of the latter decision and an affirmation of the District Court judgment in the Supreme Court. The principal contention made before this tribunal was that there was not sufficient evidence before the Commission to sustain its order of reparation, and germane to this, and vigorously insisted upon by counsel, were objections to the type of evidence admitted by the Commission. Much of the evidence was hearsay. The only witness sworn was the assistant secretary of a Cattle Raisers' Association who had gathered the data upon which the claims were based, and prepared the claims, examining the books and records of the commission merchants.[10] A tabulation was prepared, summarizing for each carrier the claims

[6] 227 U. S. 88, 93 (1912).

[7] Citing Interstate Commerce Commission *v.* Baird, IV A *supra*.

[8] Though the contention of the government was thus overruled, the court nevertheless held that the record showed substantial evidence to support the order of the Commission. [9] 253 U. S. 117 (1920).

[10] It seems that most of the actual shippers, the alleged assignors, relied upon commission houses for their book-keeping, and that the commission houses, the consignees of the cattle, made it a practice, on receiving a ship-

CHAP. IV] THE RULES OF EVIDENCE 23

as made up, and this was submitted to the respective carriers for checking. This evidence was all hearsay and was not offered as within any of the conventional exceptions to the hearsay rule. There was, furthermore, no formal proof of the handwriting of the assignors by subscribing witnesses, or otherwise. Despite this, the Supreme Court held that the evidence was properly received by the Commission, and that it warranted the reparation order. The court clearly recognized that the evidence in question was hearsay.[11] But the court held it admissible upon the ground that it was not objected to as such when introduced, nor during the hearing before the Commission, and would, therefore, have been admissible even in a court of law and, *a fortiori*, before an administrative tribunal. The court said:[12] "We are not here called upon to consider whether the Commission may receive and act upon hearsay evidence seasonably objected to as hearsay; but we do hold that in this case, where such evidence was introduced without objection and was substantially corroborated by original evidence clearly admissible against the parties to be affected, the Commission is not to be regarded as having acted arbitrarily, nor may its findings and order be rejected as wanting in support, simply because the hearsay evidence was considered with the rest."[13] The court moreover ruled that it was not error for the Commission to act upon the assignments without formal identification of the handwriting of the assignors, this upon the ground that there was substantial evidence to support the finding that the claims had been assigned, and that formal proof of the handwriting of the assignors was not necessary ". . . in so summary a hearing, in the absence of objection or contradiction. What was shown as to the relation of the shippers to the Association and the possession of the instruments of assignment by the representative of the Association who was prosecuting the claims gave a reasonable assurance of the genuineness of the instruments."[14] The court further held that the fact

ment, to pay the freight, sell the cattle and remit the proceeds less the freight. Such freight payments were the basis of the reparation order.

[11] It said: "It is not to be disputed that much of the evidence — including essential parts of it — is properly so characterized." (See p. 129 of 253 U. S.)

[12] Speaking through Mr. Justice Pitney, p. 131 of 253 U. S.

[13] The court cited Interstate Commerce Commission *v.* Baird, IV A *supra*, and Interstate Commerce Commission *v.* Louisville & N. R. Co., IV A *supra*, and quoted therefrom the dicta above set forth.

[14] 253 U. S. 117, 133 (1920).

that a reparation order has at most only the effect of prima facie evidence is an added reason for not binding the Commission too closely in respect of the character of the evidence it may receive or the manner in which its hearings shall be conducted. It distinguished *Interstate Commerce Commission* v. *Louisville & N. R. Co.*[15] upon the ground that in the instant case the Commission did not act upon evidence of which the carriers were not cognizant and to which they had no opportunity to reply.[16]

The next case to arise was *United States* v. *Abilene & S. R. Co.*[17] It also is a commonly quoted case for the statement [18] that "The

---

[15] IV A *supra*.

[16] The Supreme Court, as above pointed out, took pains to say that there was no objection to the hearsay or to the lack of identification of the signatures of the assignors of the claims. The Circuit Court of Appeals, on the contrary, had held that the hearsay had been objected to, that the objections were well taken, and that without such hearsay evidence there was not sufficient evidence to support the award. It had said (See 246 Fed. 1, 19): "Of course, this testimony was the worst kind of hearsay, but counsel claims that it was unobjected to, and therefore in an appellate court the objection that it was hearsay cannot be made. We are of the opinion, if the proceedings before the Commission are allowed to be conducted in an informal way, so far as the Commission is concerned counsel engaged in the conduct of such proceedings are not required to preserve and protect their rights with the watchful nicety that would be required in courts of justice."

The objections to the evidence at the Commission hearing were not taken with the formality and in the specific manner required in courts of law. Therefore, in view of the ruling in the Supreme Court, Spiller *v.* Atchison, Topeka & Santa Fe Ry. is authority not only for the proposition that if incompetent testimony is not objected to as such, it may be received and acted upon by an administrative tribunal, but also for the proposition that the rules of procedure concerning the taking of objections to incompetent testimony will be enforced with full vigor. It at first seems somewhat harsh and illogical, on the one hand to free the commissions and parties from the formalities of courts in respect to presentation of evidence, but upon the other to impose upon parties and their counsel the strictest precision with respect to taking objections to evidence. But it is probably sound to insist in administrative tribunals, as well as in courts, upon formality in taking objections, both for the purpose of calling fully to the attention of the tribunal the objectionable matter, and to prevent appeals and reversals upon afterthought objections by the losing party. (See Volume 18, Cases and Points for 253 U. S. Supreme Court Reports, at p. 392 of the Transcript of Record, for comment of Sanborn, Circuit Judge; and see in the same volume the Brief for Defendants in Error, at pp. 12 *et seq.*, 26 *et seq.*, 42 *et seq.*, and 49 *et seq.*, for discussion of the objections to the evidence; and see pp. 233 to 282, inclusive, of the Transcript of Record, for the objections themselves as made by counsel for the carriers.)

[17] 265 U. S. 274 (1924).   [18] *Idem*, 288.

CHAP. IV] THE RULES OF EVIDENCE 25

mere admission by an administrative tribunal of matter which under the rules of evidence applicable to judicial proceedings would be deemed incompetent does not invalidate its order." [19] But in the Abilene case the court went on to state: [20] "But a finding without evidence is beyond the power of the Commission. Papers in the Commission's files are not always evidence in a case.[21] . . . Nothing can be treated as evidence which is not introduced as such." [22] This is the real holding of the case. An Interstate Commerce Commission finding and order reducing divisions of joint rates between fourteen railroads rested in part, and as to essential facts, upon data taken from annual reports filed with the commission by the carriers pursuant to law. They were not put formally in evidence, except through excerpts, but were nevertheless used as evidence by the commission of facts which it was deemed necessary to prove. A rule of practice of the Commission [23] declared that the "Commission will take notice of items in tariffs and annual or other periodical reports of carriers properly on file. . . ." [24] The contention of the Commission was that because its examiner gave notice that it would be necessary to refer to the annual reports of the carriers, this rule " . . . permitted matter in the reports to be used as freely as if the data had been formally introduced in evidence." [25]

In *Western Paper Makers' Chemical Co.* v. *United States*,[26] in an appeal to the Supreme Court of the United States from the refusal of the District Court of Michigan to enjoin or modify orders of the Interstate Commerce Commission establishing certain through rates, it was urged, *inter alia*, that evidence was improperly considered.[27] But the court held: "These objections we have no

---

[19] For this it cites Interstate Commerce Commission v. Baird, IV A *supra*, and Spiller v. Atchison, Topeka & Santa Fe Ry., IV A *supra*, and also United States *ex rel*. Bilokumsky v. Tod, cited and discussed IV E (1) *infra* in connection with alien deportation hearings.

[20] Speaking through Mr. Justice Brandeis, p. 288 of 265 U. S.

[21] Citing the New England Divisions Case, 261 U. S. 184, 198, note 19.

[22] Citing Interstate Commerce Commission v. Louisville & N. R. Co., IV A *supra*.

[23] Rule XIII. It was altered after the decision.

[24] 265 U. S. 274, 288, note 12 (1924).

[25] *Idem*, 287.   [26] 271 U. S. 268 (1926).

[27] Neither the nature of the evidence, nor the specific objections thereto, appear in the opinion. An examination of the record in the case indicates that the matter objected to was two eleven-page exhibits showing the chronological history of specifics on rosin — the commodity upon which through rates

occasion to discuss. . . . [28] In making its determinations the Commission is not hampered by mechanical rules governing the weight or effect of evidence. The mere admission of matter which under the rules of evidence applicable to judicial proceedings would be deemed incompetent does not invalidate its order." [29]

In *Montrose Oil Refining Co.* v. *St. Louis-San Francisco R. Co.*,[30] the Interstate Commerce Commission had found that rates collected from the plaintiff for petroleum shipments over the defendants' railway lines, in so far as they exceeded 19.5 cents prior to a given date, and 26.5 cents thereafter, were unreasonable, and had awarded damages to the amount of the difference between the charges so collected and the reasonable rate of 19 cents fixed for the future. The plaintiff then filed a motion with the Commission suggesting that the reasonable rate for the future should be applied to the reparation award on the basis of 15.5 cents prior and 19 cents subsequent to the given date above referred to. This suggestion was adopted and orders entered by the Commission for payment of the award, and, defendants failing to comply, plaintiff brought suit in the District Court of the United States for Texas to recover the award. It was contended that the award was illegal because contrary to "judicial" admissions and evidence of the plaintiff before the Commission, and colloquies between the parties before the Commission's examiner and statements of plaintiff's witnesses concerning the case were urged in support of this. Reference to the briefs in the case [31] indicates that the "judicial" admissions referred to were on the part of the traffic manager, the

had been made — and on turpentine, which were admitted only for the purpose of showing the historical and chronological situation of the specifics, and which were consequently not proper to be considered, it was urged, for any other purpose. See Volume 24, Records and Briefs for 271 U. S. Court Reports, at pp. 19 and 30 of Plaintiffs' Brief, and at pp. 12 and 13 of Brief for the Interstate Commerce Commission; and see, in the same volume, Transcript of Record, 140–141. It is to be noted that it is not unusual for courts, even in jury trials, to admit evidence competent for one purpose under instructions to disregard it for all others.

[28] Speaking again through Mr. Justice Brandeis, p. 271 of 271 U. S.

[29] Citing United States *v.* Abilene & S. R. Co., IV A *supra*.

[30] 25 F. (2d) 750 (1927) aff'd. 755 (C. C. A. 5th, 1928) certiorari denied 277 U. S. 598 (1928).

[31] See p. 76 of Brief for the Plaintiffs in Error, The St. Louis-San Francisco Ry. Co. et al., Volume 5, Records and Briefs, U. S. C. C. A., Fifth Circuit, 25 F. (2d). See also p. 77 of the same brief, together with the references to the Transcript of Record therein made.

CHAP. IV] THE RULES OF EVIDENCE 27

principal witness for the plaintiff, who testified, "I think a reasonable rate via the Frisco would be 19.5 cents," and that the brief of the Montrose Oil Company before the Commission, itself prayed that the rate should have been 19.5 cents. Thus it was claimed that, both by the admission of the agent of the plaintiff and by the briefs, the company was bound by the 19.5 cents rate.[32] But the court held that this was an attack upon the internal methods employed by the Commission in arriving at its judgment and the soundness thereof, and said:[33] " . . . There is no occasion to discuss the facts. The Commission did not exceed it powers. It is not bound by mechanical rules in receiving or giving effect to the weight of evidence. Its orders are not invalidated by its refusal or failure to adhere to the strict rules of evidence obtaining in the courts. The evidence hereinbefore referred to substantially sustains its findings, and they must stand here for what they are worth. . . ."[34]

In *Beaumont, S. L. & W. R. Co. v. United States*,[35] suit was brought by carriers in the District Court of the United States for Missouri to set aside an order of the Interstate Commerce Commission prescribing a new basis for divisions of joint rates between carriers made respondents in a proceeding which had been brought by the Interstate Commerce Commission on its own motion. The Commission had found that the divisions in effect in the territory and between the roads involved were unreasonable and fixed a new basis for the division. In considering the scope of limitation of the court's jurisdiction to review the validity of the order, the District Court [36] said: "The Commission is not required to conform to the rules governing the weight or effect of evidence, and the admission of evidence, which in judicial proceedings would be incompetent, does not invalidate its orders. . . ."[37] It was contended by the carriers that the Commission had prescribed a rate prorate based on percentages of first-class rates under a so-called "southwestern rate scale," and that such scale was not in evidence. The Commis-

[32] Allegations in the complaint, and a statement of the plaintiff's president on the witness stand, were also relied on.
[33] Speaking through Wilson, District Judge, p. 754 of 25 F. (2d).
[34] Citing Western Paper Makers' Chemical Co. *v.* United States, IV A *supra*.
[35] 36 F. (2d) 789 (1929) *aff'd*. 282 U. S. 74 (1930).
[36] Speaking through Gardner, Circuit Judge, p. 793 of 36 F. (2d).
[37] Citing, *inter alia*, Western Paper Makers' Chemical Co. *v.* United States, IV A *supra*.

sion, itself, had said in respect to this:[38] "This criticism rests upon a misunderstanding of what we did. Our formula [39] was merely a method of adjusting the divisions of what we believed upon the evidence, to be a fair approximation of difference in conditions in the two territories. . . ." But it was the contention of the carriers that the Commission had no authority to use the scale even as a mechanical device or formula or method for dividing the rates without first notifying the southwestern carriers of its intention so to do. The District Court held that the decision was not bottomed upon the southwestern scale, and that the contention was without merit. Thus, the decision approves of the use of a formula or device as a part of the method of adjusting the divisions of rates without having such device in evidence. The affirmation of this case in the Supreme Court does not expressly discuss this objection to the use of the "southwestern rate scale," and both the decision in the District Court and the affirmation are made without reference in this connection to *Interstate Commerce Commission* v. *Louisville & N. R. Co.*[40] or to *United States* v. *Abilene & S. R. Co.*,[41] to which cases it seems *contra*.[42] It was further charged in this case that the decision of the Commission was based on such incompetent and unreliable evidence and conjectures as to render it void, and in this respect the District Court said that it was true that the Commission frankly admitted that it could not reach a definite statement of the relative cost of handling the particular traffic involved, but that " . . . This was an impossibility which should not, however, deprive the Commission of its authority and duty to act. The Commission considered all the facts of record, which presumably were such facts as could be submitted by either group, and if the facts were not more definite it was due to the character of the testimony presented. . . . It presumably gave proper consideration to all the facts adduced, and based upon these facts it rendered its de-

[38] See p. 799 of 36 F. (2d).
[39] The "southwestern rate scale."
[40] IV A *supra*.
[41] *Ibid.*
[42] The nature of the so-called "southwestern rate scale" is not clearly disclosed in the opinion, nor does the record clarify the matter much further. Apparently, however, it was a mileage scale of first-class rates between points in the southwestern territory which was prescribed in the Consolidated Southwestern Cases, 123 I. C. C. 203. See Volume 6, Records and Briefs for 282 U. S. Sup. Ct. Reports, and therein p. 92 *et seq.* of Appellant's Brief and p. 46 *et seq.* of Brief for the Interstate Commerce Commission.

cision. It is not suggested that more definite, satisfactory, or persuasive evidence could have been offered. The Commission in its reports says: 'Obviously it is impossible to employ any mathematical formula which will operate with precision, and it is necessary to be guided by general judgment after considering and weighing as well as we can the evidence before us.' This we take it properly describes the duty of the Commission, and presumably nobody was better qualified to act upon the evidence than this Commission, with its expert knowledge and 'national vision.' As has already been noted, the Commission is not bound by technical rules of procedure or evidence, and it is not expected nor required that its decisions can be tested by any mathematically correct rules. It was therefore not incumbent upon the Commission to produce a definite, positive statement of the difference in cost of handling traffic in the two territories involved. Neither was it essential that it state the exact differences in the traffic density and weight to be attached thereto, but the Commission is endowed with power and authority to consider and weigh all the evidence, facts, and circumstances, apply its expert knowledge and experience to the situation, and reach a conclusion and judgment based thereon."[43]

The last of the eight cases above alluded to is *Pennsylvania R. Co.* v. *United States*.[44] Here the Interstate Commerce Commission had granted a certificate of convenience and necessity to a railroad for a certain extension. While this was under construction, the railroad applied for, and was granted, another certificate for a branch from the same extension. In an action in equity by an intervening competing carrier, which contended that it was adequately serving the intended branch-line territory, to enjoin construction of the branch, upon the ground that there was no competent evidence before the Commission to sustain the second certificate, it was held that it was proper in the hearing on the second certificate for the Commission to consider the information gained in the previous hearing relating to the extension itself, to which hearing the protesting railroad was a party. The case thus holds that evidence in a previous hearing between the same parties, in a different cause, but upon a related issue, may be considered by an administrative tribunal — a departure from the rules of evidence. The case, however, is not in terms decided upon

[43] 36 F. (2d) 789, 801 (1929).
[44] 40 F. (2d) 921 (Dist. Ct. Pa., 1930).

the ground that the rules of evidence are to be differently applied by an administrative tribunal than by a court.[45]

A survey of the Interstate Commerce Commission cases thus discloses but four [46] which directly sanction the relaxation of the rules of evidence by the Commission, and of these the most carefully considered one [47] does so upon the theory that the objectionable evidence was not objected to.

But these cases and the dicta in the other four have set a pattern, which, summarized, may be said to be that the Interstate Commerce Commission is not to be too narrowly constrained by the "technical" and "narrow rules" which prevail at common law trials,[48] or by the "strict rules" prevailing in suits between private parties,[49] or by the rules which in judicial proceedings would make matter incompetent,[50] or by "mechanical rules,"[51] or by "mathematically correct rules,"[52] and these cases, particularizing, sanction the use of hearsay and of unidentified signatures,[53] the disregard of admissions of parties,[54] the use of a formula or method of adjusting rate divisions which is not in evidence,[55] and of evidence in another cause.[56] But these cases also, it is to be noted, require the production of relevant testimony and docu-

[45] In addition to the cases above discussed mention should also be made of the New England Divisions Case, wherein the United States Supreme Court held that it was proper for the Interstate Commerce Commission to base an order directing an increase, in divisions of joint through rates involving some six hundred carriers, to the New England lines " . . . upon evidence which the Commission assumed was typical in character, and ample in quantity, to justify the finding made in respect to each division of each rate of every carrier." (See 261 U. S. 184, 196 [1923]). The language is that of Mr. Justice Brandeis. But the case seems, on close scrutiny, to have to do with the weight of evidence, not with its admissibility, form, or trustworthiness.

[46] Spiller v. Atchison, Topeka & Santa Fe Ry., Western Paper Makers' Chemical Co. v. United States, Beaumont, S. L. & W. R. Co. v. United States, and Pennsylvania R. Co. v. United States, all IV A *supra*.

[47] Spiller v. Atchison, Topeka & Santa Fe Ry.

[48] Interstate Commerce Commission v. Baird, IV A *supra*.

[49] Interstate Commerce Commission v. Louisville & N. R. Co., IV A *supra*.

[50] United States v. Abilene & S. R. Co., IV A *supra*.

[51] Western Paper Makers' Chemical Co. v. United States, and Montrose Oil Refining Co. v. St. Louis-San Francisco R. Co., both IV A *supra*.

[52] Beaumont, S. L. & W. R. Co. v. United States, IV A *supra*.

[53] Spiller v. Atchison, Topeka & Santa Fe Ry., IV A *supra*.

[54] Montrose Oil Refining Co. v. St. Louis-San Francisco R. Co., IV A *supra*.

[55] Beaumont, S. L. & W. R. Co. v. United States, IV A *supra*.

[56] Pennsylvania R. Co. v. United States, IV A *supra*.

CHAP. IV] THE RULES OF EVIDENCE 31

ments,[57] forbid the use of the Commission's own information not formally proved at the hearing,[58] or the use of anything as evidence which is not introduced as such, — here data taken from annual reports filed by carriers,[59] — and assert that "the more liberal the practice in admitting testimony, the more imperative the obligation to preserve the essential rules of evidence by which rights are asserted or defended."[60]

The pattern set by these cases has been followed, as will be seen, by the courts, federal and state, in cases relating to other tribunals, especially in respect to relaxation of the rules of evidence. The limitations above set forth are not always adhered to.

B. *Federal Trade Commission.* In but one case, *John Bene & Sons, Inc.* v. *Federal Trade Commission,*[61] has a court passed upon the omission by the Federal Trade Commission to apply the rules of evidence. The Commission had ordered John Bene & Sons, who made and sold hydrogen peroxide, to desist from circulating statements, found by the Commission to be false, concerning "Daxol," a competing preparation. At the hearing the Commission took the opinion evidence of a lay witness as to the uses of the two solutions, permitted the same witness, who became a stockholder and director of the Daxol Corporation after " . . . this trouble arose . . . " and " . . . operated the books of the company . . .," to testify to antecedent events not within her knowledge, allowed this same witness to testify to correspondence antedating her connection and as to the contents of books never produced; and the Commission took testimony concerning the chemical contents of a solution supposed to be, but not identified as, "Daxol." Upon a petition to review the order to desist, question was raised as to whether the Commission was restricted to the taking of legally competent and relevant testimony. The court held that it was not. It said: "We incline to think that it is not by the statute, and, having regard to the exigencies of administrative law, that it should not be so restricted. We are of the opinion that evidence or testimony, even though legally incompetent, if of the kind that usually affects fair-minded men in the conduct of their daily and more important affairs, should be received and consid-

[57] Interstate Commerce Commission *v.* Baird, IV A *supra.*
[58] Interstate Commerce Commission *v.* Louisville & N. R. Co., IV A *supra.*
[59] United States *v.* Abilene & S. R. Co., IV A *supra.*
[60] Interstate Commerce Commission *v.* Louisville & N. R. Co., IV A *supra.*
[61] 299 Fed. 468 (C. C. A. 2d, 1924).

ered; but it should be fairly done."[62] The case thus sanctions, if it "be fairly done," the receipt and consideration of the testimony of a lay witness upon an expert question, and hearsay, secondary, and (because not connected) immaterial evidence.[63]

C. *State Public Service Commissions.* For convenience and as a matter of interest in respect to the development of the viewpoint of the courts, the cases under this topic will be discussed in the order of their decision, except that cases within a given state will be discussed together.

The case of *Steenerson* v. *Great Northern Ry. Co.*,[64] in Minnesota, is apparently the earliest public service commission case to sanction departure from the rules of evidence. It involves, in its comment, the fundamental rule that evidence to be acted upon must be introduced, so that the parties may know, cross-examine and rebut it. The Minnesota Railroad & Warehouse Commission, after a hearing, had reduced the rates on farm products of the Great Northern Railway. On appeal to the state district court the order was reversed. From an order denying a motion for a new trial, the State and the Commission appealed. The opinion does not disclose the facts underlying the comment of the court upon the question of evidence. But the question of the scope of judicial review was raised and, in defining it, the Supreme Court of Minnesota said that the Commission need not base its decision, as does a trial court, wholly upon evidence which can be submitted for review. The court stated: " . . . It is not a judicial tribunal, but an administrative body, whose powers are somewhat legislative in their character; and, like other administrative or legislative bodies, it acquires a knowledge of the facts, circumstances and conditions in its own way, and need not act on the theory that the parties should have a formal hearing on notice,[65] except so far as the statute expressly so requires."[66]

[62] 299 Fed. 468, 471 (C. C. A. 2d, 1924).
[63] On other grounds, the order of the Commission was reversed.
[64] 69 Minn. 353, 72 N. W. 713 (1897).
[65] Contrast Interstate Commerce Commission *v.* Louisville & N. R. Co., IV A *supra*, and United States *v.* Abilene & S. R. Co., IV A *supra*.
[66] The court here commented with great modesty upon the comparative abilities of commissioners and judges to deal with railroad questions: "The members of such a commission should be men of great financial ability, who have had a large amount of training and experience to fit them for their responsible and difficult duties, and they should be thoroughly familiar with the many financial and economic problems which enter into the business of con-

CHAP. IV]   THE RULES OF EVIDENCE   33

In *City of Norwalk* v. *Connecticut Co.*,[67] the Public Utilities Commission had ordered a street railway company to bear a given share of the cost of construction of a bridge. The City, burdened with the balance, appealed, first to the superior court and then to the Supreme Court of Connecticut, to question the apportionment. Certain of the grounds of the appeal [68] were objected to as treating the Public Utilities Commission as if it were a court engaged in the trial of a civil action. The appeal was allowed on other grounds, but in respect to this objection the court said: [69] " . . . Neither the Commission, nor the Superior Court on appeals from its orders, is bound by the technical rules respecting the admissibility or relevancy of evidence. So far as this case is concerned, they sit to receive aid in the formation of a personal judgment as to what is an equitable apportionment of the expense, under all the circumstances." [70]

There are two cases in Wisconsin, *Chicago & Northwestern R. Co.* v. *Railroad Commission*,[71] and *Duluth Street R. Co.* v. *Railroad Commission*.[72] In the former, in an appeal from a judgment of the circuit court affirming, in a statutory action for a review, an order of the Wisconsin Railroad Commission lowering the rate for ice

structing and operating railroads. How is a judge, who is not supposed to have any of this special learning or experience, and could not take judicial notice of it if he had it, to review the decision of commissioners, who should have it and should act upon it? It seems to us that such a judge is not fit to act in such a matter. It is not a case of the blind leading the blind, but of one who has always been deaf and blind insisting that he can see and hear better than one who has always had his eyesight and hearing, and has always used them to the utmost advantage in ascertaining the truth in regard to the matter in question. Before a judge can act intelligently in such a matter, he must have an amount of this special knowledge and experience which it will take him years to acquire. It is not sufficient that he take his first lessons from the partisan, and perhaps perjured, experts, or so-called experts, produced by the parties at the trial. He must have a broader, clearer, and surer grasp of the subject than he can get from any such unreliable lessons. We see no way of disposing of this question except to hold that on appeal from the commission the court should, to the best of their ability, take judicial notice of all such technical learning, knowledge, and information of a general character as should be known and understood by the commission. . . ." (See 69 Minn. 353, 376, 72 N. W. 713, 716.)

[67] 88 Conn. 471, 91 Atl. 442 (1914).
[68] They do not appear in the opinion.
[69] 88 Conn. 471, 479, 91 Atl. 442, 445.
[70] Citing Hopson's Appeal, 65 Conn. 140, 147, 148, 31 Atl. 531.
[71] 156 Wisc. 47, 145 N. W. 974 (1914).
[72] 161 Wisc. 245, 152 N. W. 887 (1915).

transportation within the state, and awarding reparation, it was asserted that the order was made in part upon evidence not produced before the Commission at its hearing, and not brought to the attention of the appellant railroad company, and that hence due process of law was denied. It appeared, *inter alia*, that the principal basis for computing the rate was the cost of the service to the carrier, and that this had been ascertained " . . . by the methods often explained in decisions of this Commission. . . ."[73] The "methods" referred to were those explained in previous decisions of the Commission in demonstrating the complexity of the questions investigated, the methods of arriving at the cost, and the bases of computation. It was held that reference to these decisions and the use of the methods therein stated was proper.[74] Under the local statutes, railroad companies were required to report annually to the State Board of Assessments and to the Railroad Commission upon blanks furnished by the latter, and were also required to file a freight tariff. It was held that such reports and tariffs, including those of other railroads performing like service, may be considered in arriving at the actual average cost of like service by the comparative method; that the method of ascertaining a reasonable rate by computation of the cost of service may be thus aided by comparison with what it costs other railroads,[75] and that it was not necessary that these "public documents" be formally offered in evidence before the Commission,[76] or certified up on review; that all parties know of their existence; that the Commission and court may take judicial notice of the contents, and that the parties are at liberty to present computations therefrom in argument at any stage of the litigation. In respect to the contention that the findings and order of the Commission rested upon evidence taken in the absence of and without notice to the appellant, the court said: " . . . Doubtless the Commission is not required to proceed in this as in other respects with the strict formalities which obtain in courts of common-law and equity jurisdiction. But the statute contemplates a hearing and the taking of evidence in the matter of fixing rates. . . . Nevertheless from the admin-

[73] Quoted at p. 59 of 156 Wisc. from the opinion of the Commission.
[74] Compare Beaumont, S. L. & W. R. Co. *v.* United States, IV A *supra*, in its use of the "southwestern rate scale."
[75] The Commission, so the court held, used both the actual cost of service, and the comparative, methods, in arriving at a reasonable rate.
[76] Contrast United States *v.* Abilene & S. R. Co., IV A *supra*.

istrative nature of the tribunal, the requirements of expert knowledge, the nature of the duties required, and the subjects considered, there must be a very considerable number of duties which the Commission is authorized to perform without the formality of trial or hearing or the formal taking of evidence. . . ."[77]

In the second case in Wisconsin [78] there was a hearing before the Railroad Commission resulting in reduction of street-railway fares, thereafter an action in the state circuit court to set aside the order, and a trial *de novo*, and thereafter an appeal by the carrier to the supreme court. It was alleged that the Commission had improperly considered, in arriving at the original cost of the railway property, a cost appraisal, made by engineers of the Commission, not formally offered in evidence, and not exhibited to the carrier, and that the engineers who made the appraisal were not sworn as witnesses at the hearing.[79] The court held that under its previous decision [80] this appraisal could properly be considered,[81] although [82] " . . . Of course common fairness would dictate that the plaintiff be advised of the appraisal made by the employees

---

[77] "This is true," continued the court, "of all administrative tribunals. There is also a vast amount of acquired expert knowledge which the Commission may apply to facts in evidence, as, for illustration, when the number of tons hauled and the distance hauled and the whole cost is given, what part of it usually and ordinarily represents terminal expenses; the usual proportion of terminal expenses to miles hauled; the usual and ordinary ratio of distribution of freight charges according to the value of the product carried; what allowance or increase is usually and ordinarily made for size or bulk proportionate to weight; the average number of tons carried in a car; the ordinary proportion of empty to loaded cars; the ordinary consumption of fuel per train mile or per ton mile or per passenger, and many other items of information which, while more difficult and complicated, are yet of the same nature as the expert knowledge of a farmer with reference to the number of acres which should constitute a day's plowing; a merchant with respect to the usual percentage of cost of packing and delivery; a sailor with reference to the usual number of miles which should be made in a given time and in a given direction with a given direction and velocity of wind. None of these estimates are mathematically accurate, but long practice in making estimates of that kind makes one an expert." (Pp. 55 and 56 of 156 Wisc.).

[78] 161 Wisc. 245, 152 N. W. 887 (1915).

[79] The appraisal was based upon an inventory of the railway's property made eleven years before the hearing. This inventory was obtained from the railway and was, with the appraisal, one of the files in the office of the Commission when the hearing was had.

[80] Just discussed.

[81] Contrast with United States *v.* Abilene & S. R. Co., IV A *supra*.

[82] P. 257 of 161 Wisc.

of the Commission, if the Commission intended to use such figures as a basis for decision." [83]

In *Steamboat Canal Co. v. Garson*,[84] the Public Service Commission of Nevada took into consideration, at a hearing upon the canal company water rates, evidence taken at former hearings and data on file with the Commission upon the question of the value of the ditch, this value having been fixed at the former hearings. The Commission indicated that it would consider the former evidence for this purpose and would make no change in the valuation without a new showing. It gave notice of intention to use this evidence to all parties at the outset of the hearing, and allowed opportunity to examine the proposed evidence and data. The protesting water users had urged, and the state district court had held, that for the use of this evidence the Commission's order should be reversed. But the Supreme Court of Nevada held that the hearing was not rendered a nullity. It said: [85] " . . . The consideration of the testimony and data obtained at the former hearings, after due notice that it would be submitted and considered, was an infraction of the strict rules of evidence which prevail in the trial of cases in courts of law, but administrative boards of this character are not hampered by technical procedure. True, they cannot dispense with the essential rules of evidence which conduce to a fair and impartial hearing, but from the nature of their organization and the duties imposed upon them by statute they are essentially empowered with liberal discretion in passing upon the competency of evidence. If it were otherwise, the policy of the law, in conferring authority upon the Public Service Commission to supervise and regulate the rates, would be in a large measure frustrated.[86] On the facts of this case we are not prepared to say that the action of the commission in considering the testi-

[83] The court said: "We do not understand it to be claimed that there was any intentional suppression by the Commission of evidentiary matters of this kind." (P. 257 of 161 Wisc.).

The court further stated that should it be conceded that the Commission did consider improper evidence, since the trial in the circuit court was *de novo* a mistake by the Commission in considering improper evidence could furnish no ground for reversal of the circuit court judgment. The court also said that it appeared that little reliance was placed on the inventory in arriving at a conclusion.

[84] 43 Nev. 298, 185 P. 801 (1919).

[85] 43 Nev. 298, 309, 185 P. 801, 805.

[86] Citing Interstate Commerce Commission *v.* Louisville & N. R. Co., IV A *supra*.

mony and data complained of by respondents was an abuse of discretion by the commission, or that it deprived respondents of a substantial right." The court distinguished *Interstate Commerce Commission* v. *Louisville & N. R. Co., supra,* upon the ground that therein there was no hearing, because the party involved did not know what evidence was offered or considered and was not given an opportunity to test, explain, or refute it.[87]

In *St. Louis Southwestern Ry. Co.* v. *Stewart*,[88] the Corporation Commission, in a proceeding initiated by a municipality, ordered the defendant railway company to construct a new passenger station, upon the ground that the existing building was of insufficient capacity, unsightly, unsanitary, and inconvenient. There was an inspection by the engineer of the Commission, and the report thereof was not put in evidence, either in writing or otherwise.[89] It was held that the Commission had the right to consider this report, if there were such a report, upon the ground that it would have been advisory rather than evidentiary in character, but that the report should have been put into the record had it not been for the waiver of this by the failure of the railway company to insist thereon. The appellant railway company had had the benefit "of a trial de novo in the Circuit Court on the record, which included all of the testimony which it saw fit to introduce before the Commission,"[90] and that review was not merely for errors but to determine the merits. The court [91] held that for this reason the fullest requirements of the law were satisfied.[92]

In *Williamson* v. *Railroad Commission*,[93] the California Rail-

[87] Compare Steamboat Canal Co. *v.* Garson with Pennsylvania R. Co. *v.* United States, IV A *supra.*

[88] 150 Ark. 586, 235 S. W. 1003 (1921).

[89] The record did not show that the report was in writing.

[90] 150 Ark. 586, 593, 235 S. W. 1003, 1005.

[91] Citing Ohio Valley Water Co. *v.* Ben Avon Borough, 253 U. S. 287, 40 Sup. Ct. 527, 64 L. ed. 908.

[92] In addition to the point above discussed, this case involved a personal inspection of the locus by the Commission. As to that the court held that, while the Commission may not consider matters within their personal knowledge which cannot be put into the record, nevertheless, aside from any express statutory authority, " . . . It was within the power of the Commission to make a personal inspection, not to gather evidence, but to understand that which is introduced in such form as can be put into the record for consideration on appeal. That is all that it is shown was done in this case." (See 150 Ark. 586, 592, 235 S. W. 1003, 1005.)

[93] 193 Cal. 22, 222 P. 803 (1924).

road Commission, upon application of the Natomas Water Company, and after hearing, had found and determined that it and its predecessors in interest had been from the time of organization a public utility and their waters impressed with a public use, and had thereupon ascertained the value of the company's property and established a schedule of rates in excess of those stipulated in certain contracts between the petitioners [94] and the water company. The petitioners had raised an issue that the company and its predecessors were not a public utility. Objection was made to the reception of certain evidence [95] before the Commission. The court held:[96] "Reception of testimony not strictly within the rules of evidence is not of itself a ground for the annulment of an order or decision of the commission. As was said in Brewer v. Railroad Commission, *supra*: [97] 'This is not an ordinary appeal, nor has this court the authority, under its limited powers of review, to set aside orders of the railroad commission in matters over which it has been given jurisdiction, because of errors in the admission or rejection of evidence.' If there is sufficient legal evidence to be found in the record to sustain the commission's order, the requirements of the statute are satisfied. In such a case incompetent or immaterial matter becomes mere surplusage." [98]

[94] In certiorari to review the order of the Commission.
[95] The nature of this evidence is not disclosed in the opinion.
[96] 193 Cal. 22, 35, 222 P. 803, 809.
[97] 190 Cal. 60, 210 P. 511 (1922).
[98] At the hearing in this case the Commission had received in evidence (See 193 Cal. 22, 35, 222 P. 803, 809) " . . . excerpts from findings appearing in the reports of this court and in the United States Supreme Court upon review of certain decisions on appeal from state courts in which the Natomas Water & Mining Company is defendant. These decisions review the history of the construction and the purposes of the construction of the water system . . . and tend strongly to support respondent's claim that it had been from its beginning a public utility." In respect to the admission of these excerpts, which it was alleged was improper, the court said (See 193 Cal. 22, 36, 222 P. 803, 809): "It is admitted that the findings in these cases are res inter alios acta; but it is claimed they are admissible under a well-recognized exception to the hearsay rule upon the principle that oral declarations and hearsay evidence are admissible to establish matters of general and public interest and as a means, and in many cases the only means, of proving traditionary reputation and ancient documents. Respondent's claim is not wholly without merit, but we feel satisfied that even though the matters complained of, and which were admitted in evidence, be eliminated from the record by us, we would not even then be justified in disturbing the commission's findings." The court made the remarks above quoted also applicable to an objection made to the

CHAP. IV] THE RULES OF EVIDENCE 39

In *Lindsey* v. *Pub. Util. Comm.*,[99] the reports of engineers and experts of the Ohio Public Utilities Commission were taken into consideration by the latter in a proceeding fixing the property value and rates of a telephone company. The docket entry of the Commission showed "report of telephone expert filed" on a date more than two months prior to the finding and order of the Commission. Neither such report, nor a copy thereof, had been made a part of the record on appeal to the Supreme Court of Ohio. It was held that the Ohio General Code gave the Commission power to avail itself of the services of engineers and experts,[100] and that it acted within its authority in sending them to make independent investigations as to value, operating expense and revenue, and that it was authorized to give the reports of such experts such weight as their experience, learning, thoroughness, integrity and dependability justify, provided that the parties are given opportunity to examine such reports and to cross-examine the makers thereof. And the court held that, in view of the docket entry above referred to, the plaintiffs in error in the instant case, who were attacking the rates fixed by the Commission's order, could not be heard to complain in the reviewing court that they did not know of the existence of the document filed, and that they could not complain where there had been no effort on their part to assert their rights with reference to such document in the tribunal after discovery.[101]

reception of a report made from a compilation of various reports of former superintendents of the water company's predecessors, many of whom were deceased, said reports showing the revenue derived from water charges at an early period of the system's existence. As will be seen from the above language, the court does not clearly rule upon the admissibility of the excerpts or the report.

The suggestion that such excerpts were admissible in evidence, even in an administrative tribunal, seems unique.

[99] 111 O. St. 6, 144 N. E. 729 (1924).

[100] Ohio General Code, §§ 499-8-11-15 and 614-6.

[101] In another case in Ohio, Grubb v. Public Utilities Commission, 119 O. St. 264, 163 N. E. 713, decided in 1928, and without referring to the case just discussed, the same court held that it was not improper for the Public Utilities Commission, in a hearing on application for a certificate of convenience and necessity to operate an interstate motor-bus line, to take into consideration knowledge gained by reason of former proceedings against the applicant for violation of the regulations of the Commission while operating other motor-bus lines, as bearing upon the question of the good faith of the present application, it being asserted by competing companies that the applicant was attempting to obtain the certificate for its nuisance value. The case does not discuss the rules of evidence as applied in administrative hearings, but, since the in-

40   ADMINISTRATIVE TRIBUNALS AND   [CHAP. IV

In Kansas, in *Atchison, T. & S. F. R. Co.* v. *Public Service Commission of Kansas*,[102] the Public Service Commission had granted a certificate of convenience and necessity to operate a motor-bus line. In an injunction action brought in the state district court by a competing railroad company against the Commission and the motor-bus company, the plaintiff challenged the legal sufficiency of the evidence to warrant granting the certificate. *Inter alia*, a number of letters were introduced in the hearing before the Commission, addressed to the Commission, and purporting to have been written by men occupying important business positions in cities along the proposed bus line, commending the project and those back of it, and referring in some instances to the inadequate facilities existing, and stating that the proposed line would afford transportation facilities needed by the public. Under the Kansas statutes and decisions, the district court trial was *de novo*, and the Kansas courts had held,[103] "So long as a judicial hearing *de novo* is provided, it is not very important just what sort of evidence is received by the Commission, or how it is received, if the parties concerned are apprised of it."[104] In the instant case the court held that the Commission may gather its facts in the most informal way and may and should avail itself of all reports and data gathered by its own staff of engineers, statisticians, and accountants; but it is only fair that all such facts, data, and reports, wheresoever gleaned, should be presented in public, so that the parties to be affected may show, if they can, by cross-examination or otherwise, that such data and reports are either inaccurate, fallacious, or incomplete or not of controlling significance.[105] The court sustained

formation of the Commission was apparently not placed on record, the case is in effect a sanction of a violation of the fundamental requirement that evidence acted upon must be introduced and subjected to explanation, attack and rebuttal by those adversely affected by it. The case is, therefore, to be contrasted with Interstate Commerce Commission *v.* Louisville & N. R. Co., IV A *supra*.

[102] 130 Kansas 777, 288 P. 755 (1930).

[103] 130 Kansas 777, 781, 288 P. 755, 758.

[104] Wichita R. & Light Co. *v.* Court of Industrial Relations, 113 Kansas 217, 237, 214 P. 797, 807 (1923).

[105] This requirement was upon the faith and in substantially the words of Wichita R. & Light Co. *v.* Court of Industrial Relations, *supra*, supporting a district court reversal of a commission order, in an electric power rate case, for the reason that the order of the commission was largely based, not upon the evidence presented to the commission at the public hearing, but upon the report of the commission's own engineer, of which the complaining parties

CHAP. IV] THE RULES OF EVIDENCE 41

the order of the Commission, notwithstanding the hearsay and conclusions above referred to, but, in so doing, announced [106] that it was the function of the Commission to draw its own conclusion from proof of the conditions in the territory, rather than from the consensus of opinions of witnesses upon the ultimate fact as to the existence or non-existence of the public necessity and convenience, and that, in addition to the evidence referred to, there was competent evidence to support the order. Thus, while the court sanctions the admission by an administrative tribunal of hearsay and conclusion testimony, it implies that it is upon competent evidence that the essential facts must be found.[107]

In *Schuylkill Ry. Co.* v. *Pub. Service Comm.*,[108] the violation of the best evidence rule is sanctioned by the Supreme Court of Pennsylvania. There had been a proceeding before the Public Service Commission by the plaintiff railway company for a certificate of public convenience, approving a renewal or re-location of a grade-crossing over the double tracks of the Lehigh Valley Railroad Company, and apportioning the cost of the re-location between the two. The Commission based its finding upon an alleged copy of a contract between the Lehigh Valley Railroad Company and a predecessor in interest of the plaintiff. This copy was received by the Commission's examiner over objection by the plaintiff, not to the relevancy or legal effect thereof, but upon the ground that the copy did not "come up to the proof required in a legal proceeding in the state of Pennsylvania." [109] The Commission granted the certificate approving the replacement, but directed the expense to be borne wholly by the plaintiff. On appeal to the superior court the order of the Commission was affirmed, but the present appeal was allowed and limited to the question: "Had the Public Service Commission the right to base their find-

had no notice until several weeks after the order fixing new rates as against them was made.

[106] Upon the faith and in the language of Eager v. Pub. Util. Comm., 113 O. St. 605, 149 N. E. 865 (1925).

[107] In Wichita R. & Light Co. v. Court of Industrial Relations, *supra*, the court had further said: " . . . We have said that the formalities of a judicial court need not be followed, but this is really no detriment to the parties; it facilitates the development of the facts; and it is because of the free and easy procedure permissible before the commission that a trial *de novo*, not a mere appeal, is accorded in a judicial court from the orders of the commission." (See p. 237 of 113 Kansas.)

[108] 268 Pa. 430, 112 Atl. 5 (1920), *aff'g.* 71 Pa. Super. Ct. 204.

[109] See p. 432 of 268 Pa. and p. 6 of 112 Atl.

ing on an alleged copy of a contract which was not proved in accordance with law?"[110] The supreme court held [111] that "The Public Service Company Law (Act of July 26, 1913, P. L. 1374) contains no provision relating to the kind of evidence which may be received and acted upon by the commission; but, the commissioners not being considered as judges learned in the law, the legislature necessarily did not contemplate that the strict rules of evidence should be applied to their hearings. The act, by section 18, article VI, provides that the 'testimony taken' shall come up on appeal as part of the record; this was no doubt intended to afford the courts an opportunity to see that there was some reasonable basis in the proofs for the decision of the commission, not that they might examine to see whether the strict rules of evidence had been complied with."[112] In *Hoffman* v. *Pub. Serv. Comm.*,[113] an application for a certificate of public convenience to operate taxicabs in Philadelphia was opposed by competing cab companies, and the Commission denied the application. Upon appeal by the applicants to the superior court it was contended that the Commission's order was erroneous, *inter alia*, because it considered facts within its knowledge, of which there was no evidence in the record. In making a finding upon certain issues the Commission considered evidence not formally offered, but which appeared in the records of other cases of the Commission bearing upon the taxicab situation in Philadelphia. The Commission announced at the hearing that all parties "may be under notice that the commission intends . . . to take full consideration of the history of the taxicab service in this city as revealed and divulged by the records before the commission."[114] The appellants made no protest. Later in the hearing the Commission announced that it would give consideration to all of its findings of record in matters pertaining to taxicab transportation in Philadelphia. It was held that there was no error in these respects, for the reasons that appellants knew what evidence would

[110] See p. 432 of 268 Pa. and p. 6 of 112 Atl.

[111] *Ibid.*

[112] Counsel for the Lehigh Valley Railroad Company, who introduced the copy, stated that it was taken from the files of the company's secretary in Philadelphia, where original copies of all agreements of the company were kept, and that it was prepared and verified by him. It seems probable, therefore, that the copy was reliable. Nevertheless, since the non-availability of the original was not shown, the rules of evidence would exclude the exhibit.

[113] 99 Pa. Super. Ct. 417, 428 (1930).

[114] See p. 427 of 99 Pa. Super. Ct.

CHAP. IV]   THE RULES OF EVIDENCE   43

be considered by the Commission and that mere admission by an administrative tribunal of matters which, under the rules of evidence applicable to judicial proceedings, would be deemed incompetent, does not invalidate an order made by it. The court said: " . . . All parties must be fully apprised of the evidence submitted or to be considered, and must be given opportunity to cross-examine witnesses, to inspect documents and to offer evidence in explanation or rebuttal. . . . But an administrative tribunal may take notice of results reached by it in other cases, when its doing so is made to appear in the record and the facts thus noted are specified so that matters of law are saved. In view of . . . the attitude of acquiescence of counsel for appellants [115] . . . we are not persuaded that it was reversible error for the commission to treat these records as evidence in the case and ground certain findings of fact upon them."[116] The court also held that the findings made upon the evidence objected to were merely collateral to the crucial question before the Commission as to whether the proposed service was "necessary or proper for the service, accommodation, convenience or safety of the public."[117]

[115] And in view of authorities cited, to wit: Tagg Bros. & Moorehead v. United States, 280 U. S. 420, 34 L. ed. 287, 294 (correctly 74 L. ed. 524) (1930), Schuylkill Ry. Co. v. Pub. Serv. Comm., just discussed, United States v. B. & O. Southwestern Ry., 226 U. S. 14, 57 L. ed. 104 (1912), Steamboat Canal Co. v. Garson, IV C supra.

[116] 99 Pa. Super. Ct. 417, 428.

[117] In City of Huntington et al. v. Public Serv. Commission, 101 W. Va. 378, 133 S. E. 144 (1926), there was admitted in evidence by the Public Service Commission, in a hearing upon telephone rates in connection with the Commission's determination of the risks and uncertainties of the investments of the telephone company as compared with other business investments in West Virginia, as bearing upon the return which the business should produce to command necessary credit and accumulate a proper surplus after payment of interest and other expenses, an excerpt from a speech of the president of the Bell Telephone Securities Company delivered before the Investment Bankers Association of America, showing that the applicant telephone company, seeking increased rates, had the financial support and managerial supervision of the Securities Company, with its vast resources and highly developed organization. The City of Huntington and others petitioned for a suspension of the Commission's order allowing the increased rates, and the telephone company cross-assigned error. No error was assigned by the telephone company upon the introduction by the protestants of this evidence, and the case does not, therefore, expressly pass upon its admissibility; but the order of the Commission was sustained, and the case thus impliedly sanctions its use and illustrates the wide departure from the rules of evidence which administrative

By way of summary of the State Public Service Commission cases it may be noted that the tribunals are by the reviewing courts freed from application of the "strict" rules of evidence,[118] that they may take testimony "not strictly within the rules of evidence" and will not be held accountable for "mere errors in admission or rejection,"[119] that they are not bound by the "technical rules" respecting admissibility or relevancy,[120] not required to proceed with the "strict formalities" which obtain in courts of common law and equity jurisdiction.[121] The tribunals may acquire knowledge of facts "in their own way and need not act upon the theory that parties are entitled to a formal hearing on notice";[122] and facts may be gathered "in the most informal way" and it is "not very important what evidence is received" if there is a *de novo* hearing on review.[123]

Some of the cases, as noted, go so far, seemingly, as to dispense with the introduction of evidence, and this without stated limitation;[124] others dispense with introduction but require the commission by way of "common fairness" to advise the parties of the matter considered by the commission [125] or do so where the parties know of the matter in question and have opportunity to test, ex-

tribunals make. The excerpt is, of course, a violation of the hearsay rule and of the rule that an expert's qualifications must be shown.

In connection with the foregoing cases involving violation of the rules of evidence by administrative tribunals, the case of People *v.* Public Service Commission of Second Dist. of New York, 127 App. Div. 480, 112 N. Y. Supp. 133 (1908), is of interest. It holds that relevant evidence must be admitted by a board of railroad commissioners in a hearing to determine whether an alleged railroad company was duly incorporated and in connection therewith whether the required ten per cent of the minimum amount of capital stock had been subscribed and paid in good faith. The commission had excluded evidence tending to show that a deposit made in a bank to the credit of directors was not, in fact, a bona fide corporation fund. Held, error. Compare with Interstate Commerce Commission *v.* Baird, IV A *supra.*

[118] Steamboat Canal Co. *v.* Garson, and Schuylkill Ry. *v.* Pub. Serv. Comm., both IV C *supra.*

[119] Williamson *v.* Railroad Commission, IV C *supra.*

[120] City of Norwalk *v.* Connecticut Co., IV C *supra.*

[121] Chicago & Northwestern R. Co. *v.* Railroad Commission, and Duluth St. R. Co. *v.* Railroad Commission, both IV C *supra.*

[122] Steenerson *v.* Great Northern Ry. Co., IV C *supra.*

[123] Atchison, T. & S. F. R. Co. *v.* Public Service Commission of Kansas, IV C *supra.*

[124] Steenerson *v.* Great Northern Ry. Co., IV C *supra.*

[125] Duluth St. R. Co. *v.* Railroad Commission, IV C *supra.*

CHAP. IV] THE RULES OF EVIDENCE 45

plain or refute it.[126] Some of the courts open wide the evidential gates in the tribunal hearings because they are closed again in trials *de novo* on review.[127]

One of the courts, however, requires that everything be presented in public and that there must be competent evidence upon which to find the essential facts,[128] and another warrants departure from the "strict rules" if there is "a reasonable basis in the proofs" for the commission's decision,[129] and still another requires sufficient "legal" evidence in addition to the "surplusage" of incompetent and immaterial matter to support the commission's decision.[130] One court,[131] though sanctioning the use of an expert's report filed with the commission, requires that the parties have opportunity to examine the report and to cross-examine the maker.[132]

The kinds of evidence received in violation of the rules of evidence are commonly hearsay in the form of carriers' reports,[133] commissioners' and engineers' reports,[134] testimony and data in other causes,[135] and letters.[136] Such evidence of course usually also violates the rule against the receipt of conclusions or opinions except through the lips of experts whose qualifications have been

[126] Steamboat Canal Co. v. Garson, and Hoffman v. Pub. Serv. Comm., both IV C *supra*. In the latter case there was acquiescence by the parties; in the former the court insisted upon preservation of the "essential rules" which conduce to a fair hearing.

[127] St. Louis Southwestern Ry. Co. v. Stewart, IV C *supra*. In this case the material objected to was "advisory" rather than "evidential," and the court, though sanctioning a "view" said in a dictum that the Commission cannot act upon personal knowledge not put into the record. Atchison T. & S. F. R. Co. v. Public Service Commission of Kansas, IV C *supra*.

[128] Atchison T. & S. F. R. Co. v. Public Service Commission of Kansas, IV C *supra*.

[129] Schuylkill Ry. Co. v. Pub. Service Comm., IV C *supra*.

[130] Williamson v. Railroad Commission, IV C *supra*.

[131] Lindsey v. Pub. Util. Comm. of Ohio, IV C *supra*.

[132] Note also that the United States Supreme Court, speaking through Mr. Justice Brandeis, refuses to sanction orders based upon findings made upon evidence which because irrelevant and inaccurate does not support them. Northern Pacific Ry. Co. v. Department of Public Works, 268 U. S. 39 (1925).

[133] Chicago & Northwestern R. Co. v. Railroad Commission, IV C *supra*.

[134] Duluth St. R. Co. v. Railroad Commission; St. Louis Southwestern Ry. Co. v. Stewart; Lindsey v. Pub. Util. Comm. of Ohio, all IV C *supra*.

[135] Steamboat Canal Co. v. Garson; Grubb v. Public Utilities Commission; Hoffman v. Pub. Serv. Comm., all IV C *supra*.

[136] Atchison T. & S. F. R. Co. v. Public Service Commission of Kansas, IV C *supra*.

subjected to the test of cross-examination. There was, as noted, one violation of the best evidence rule.[137]

D. *Taxation.* The cases here collected are appeals from administrative rulings in assessment, abatement and equalization hearings, where the rules of evidence have not been applied and where point has been made of that on appeal in the state courts. Cases were found only in Massachusetts, Illinois, Nebraska, New Hampshire and New York.

In Massachusetts the City of Lowell, in *Lowell* v. *Commissioners of Middlesex County*,[138] appealed from a tax abatement by county commissioners and urged, *inter alia*, that it was error for them at the abatement hearing to receive in evidence their own return of their proceedings in a similar case between the same parties and in respect to the same property for the previous year. This was offered in connection with testimony that if there were any change in the property during the intervening period it was by way of depreciation. The court held that this was not error; that the evidence was admissible as the opinion of the same commissioners upon value a year before; that such a board may inform itself in any reasonable manner of many circumstances which may affect the judgment of any member; and that so long as it does not adopt wrong standards of value its proceedings ought not to be set aside because of consideration of [139] "evidence which a court would not admit." [140]

In Illinois, in *Pratt* v. *Raymond*,[141] in an action in equity to enjoin the collection of a tax on the complainant's property, levied upon an assessment entered by a statutory board, it was urged that the proceedings of the board were irregular in that it acted upon evidence obtained by its members in secrecy from complainant's business rivals, and upon evidence of his commercial rating, and upon unsworn testimony; that is to say, hearsay and secret

[137] Schuylkill Ry. Co. *v.* Pub. Serv. Comm., IV C *supra.*
[138] 152 Mass. 372, 25 N. E. 469, second case (1890).
[139] 152 Mass. 372, 380, 25 N. E. 469, 472.
[140] In Lake Co. *v.* Laconia, 68 N. H. 284, 35 Atl. 252 (1895), the Supreme Court of New Hampshire sanctioned the consideration by city assessors, in fixing the value of certain property, of a judicial determination of the value thereof for the previous year. This, it was said, narrowed the field of investigation to any increase or decrease during the year. The court did not discuss the rules of evidence.
[141] 188 Ill. 469, 58 N. E. 16 (1900).

CHAP. IV]   THE RULES OF EVIDENCE   47

evidence were complained of. The Supreme Court of Illinois affirmed dismissal of the bill.[142]

In Nebraska, in *Western Union Tel. Co.* v. *Dodge County*,[143] the valuation of the property of the Western Union Telegraph Company was raised by the county board of supervisors to a figure above the one returned by the Company, and this was done upon the testimony of an expert accountant who based his computation as to stock and bond values upon Poor's Manual and other standard publications. Upon appeal to the supreme court from a district court judgment sustaining this action [144] the court held that such evidence was properly received. It said: "Assessors and equalization boards must act upon the best and most reliable information at their command. Poor's Manual is resorted to by the commercial world as an authority upon the amount and value of the stocks and bonds of the several leading corporations in this country, and whatever is good evidence for those dealing in such stocks and bonds cannot be regarded as either immaterial or incompetent for the taxing authorities to act upon. Boards of equalization are not governed in their investigation of the values of taxable property by the strict rules of evidence applied by courts of law in the trial of ordinary cases, and upon appeal from their findings the court may receive evidence of any pertinent fact tending to show the true value of the property."[145]

In New York, in *People* v. *Hicks*,[146] in certiorari by a railroad to review a tax assessment, it was urged as error that reports of the railroad, required by law to be filed, were considered by the assessors. The court upheld this, saying: " . . . they furnish almost the only available means of testing earning capacity. The assessors had a right to refer to them, and probably did, and the peculiar character of the proceeding seems to make them *ex necessitate* a source and means of information. To apply rigidly all the rules of evidence to such an investigation might make it fruitless."[147] The

[142] The Illinois Commerce Commission is forbidden by statute to act upon secret evidence: "In all cases in which the Commission bases any action on reports of investigations or inquiries not conducted as hearings, such reports shall be made a part of the records of the Commission." Ill. Rev. Stat. (Cahill, 1931) c. 111a, § 79.   [143] 80 Neb. 18, 113 N. W. 805 (1907).

[144] The district court lowered the figure set by the board of review, but left it still above the original return.

[145] 80 Neb. 18, 21, 113 N. W. 805, 807.

[146] 105 N. Y. 198, 11 N. E. 653 (Court of Appeals of N. Y., 1887).

[147] 105 N. Y. 198, 201, 11 N. E. 653, 654.

opinion does not make it clear how the reports were used, that is, whether merely referred to, or introduced at the hearing; apparently, however, the former. If so, the case sanctions the use of information not put in evidence. If introduced, the case supports hearsay and self-serving matter.[148] In *People ex rel. Schabacker* v. *State Assessors*,[149] the state assessors reduced, in favor of a certain town, the equalization by the supervisors, of county taxes, and credited that town and ordered the reduction allocated to other towns. In certiorari proceedings in the supreme court, at the instance of a supervisor of one of the other towns, it was urged as error that the state assessors in their hearing admitted in evidence deeds to lands, upon the theory that the consideration therein named was evidence of the value of the parcels conveyed. The statutes [150] directed the assessors to "prepare rules and regulations in relation to bringing such appeals [151] and the hearing or trial thereof." [152] The supreme court held that the legislature had in mind a summary review by the state assessors and that it was proper for the legislature to authorize proof by affidavit, or in such other form as the assessors might prescribe, and that " . . . To have adopted the rule that hearings before the assessors should be governed by rules in force in trial of actions before courts, would necessarily have resulted in protracted and expensive litigation, and therefore it was provided that the assessors should make the rules and regulations governing the bringing of appeals and the hearing or trial thereof,"[153] and, further, that the state assessors " . . . are a subordinate and an administrative tribunal . . . and not a court limited in its functions, within the provisions of the constitution. Their action must be considered, having in view the special powers conferred, and the purposes for which their organization was intended, and not confined by the application of strict rules which prevail in reference to trials and proceedings in courts of law." [154] The assessors had determined in their rules to receive evidence of the character of that objected to, and there was in addition to this other competent evidence. Therefore, the action

[148] Unless the reports were admissions, which does not appear.
[149] 47 Hun 450 (N. Y. 1888).
[150] Chapter 49, Laws of 1876.
[151] To the assessors from the equalization by the county supervisors.
[152] 47 Hun (N. Y.) 450, 453.
[153] 47 Hun (N. Y.) 450, 454.
[154] *Ibid.*

CHAP. IV] THE RULES OF EVIDENCE 49

of the assessors was affirmed.[155] *People ex rel. Hunt* v. *Priest* [156] was a similar case. The determination of the state board of assessors reviewing equalization by a county board of supervisors was challenged on the ground, *inter alia*, that it received in evidence affidavits of assessors of the various towns concerned, in explanation of the contents of another exhibit [157] without producing the affiants for cross-examination. The statutes here were similarly worded to those upon which the decision in *People ex rel. Schabacker* v. *State Assessors* [158] was based. Previous statutes had expressly authorized the use of affidavits. It was held that their use was proper. The court said: [159] "The respondents' answer to this first ground of challenge is that this review by the state board is not such a judicial proceeding as requires the application of the rules of evidence which hold in a court of law. This answer we think sufficient. In the first place, the proceeding is one in which it would be impracticable to apply the strict legal rules of evidence. Individual property rights are affected only indirectly through the tax which must ultimately be paid upon the equalized valuation. The review upon appeal from the determination of the board of supervisors, though primarily a right of appeal only, is nevertheless in the nature of an original investigation. The question to be determined involves, to an extent, the value of every piece of real property in the county. To establish those valuations by evidence admissible only in a court of law would make the proceeding so cumbersome as to make it practically impossible to prosecute, and

[155] It had been held in People *ex rel.* the Board of Supervisors of Chenango Co. *v.* The Board of State Assessors, 22 Weekly Dig. 453 (N. Y. Sup. Court, 1885), that the courts are not to review the rulings of the Board of State Assessors in admitting and rejecting evidence. The instant case refused to go this far, stating that such a rule carried to its fullest extent would authorize the Board to refuse arbitrarily to receive any evidence which might be offered, and would render the court powerless to review the arbitrary action of the Board in refusing to receive competent and material evidence. The instant case held that a refusal to receive evidence absolutely essential to the protection of either of the parties, would constitute an erroneous ruling of law affecting the rights of the parties within subdivision 3 of section 2140, Code of Civil Procedure, providing that on certiorari it shall be determined whether any rule of law affecting the rights of the parties has been violated to their prejudice by the Board of State Assessors.

[156] 90 App. Div. 520, 85 N. Y. Supp. 481 (1904).
[157] A schedule of recorded conveyances.   [158] Just discussed.
[159] Speaking through Mr. Justice Smith, p. 522 of 90 App. Div., and p. 483 of 85 N. Y. Supp.

so costly as to take from the town all benefit of a favorable adjudication."[160] In *People ex rel. Empire Mortgage Co.* v. *Cantor* [161] it was held that there was such a hearing upon the merits of an application to tax commissioners to reduce taxes as will constitute a waiver by the commissioners, who resisted an appeal from the refusal to reduce, of objections to matters of form and procedure, notwithstanding the fact that testimony was not taken under oath. "On such a hearing," said the court,[162] "the rigid rules of evidence do not apply; they may take the unsworn statement of an agent or attorney." [163]

Thus the cases reviewing the departure from the rules of evidence at tax assessment, abatement, and equalization hearings warrant the receipt of evidence "which a court would not admit,"[164] free the commissions from the "strict rules,"[165] or from the "rigid rules,"[166] of evidence applied in courts, or indicate that "to apply rigidly all the rules of evidence . . . might make . . . such hearings . . .

[160] People *ex rel.* Schabacker v. State Assessors, *supra*, was cited, and its discussion of the statutes relating to the reviews in question relied on.

[161] 190 App. Div. 512, 180 N. Y. Supp. 139 (1920).

[162] Speaking through Mr. Justice Page, p. 516 of 190 App. Div., and p. 142 of 180 N. Y. Supp.

[163] In People *ex rel.* American Mfg. Co. *v.* Gifford, 134 Misc. 487, 235 N. Y. Supp. 578 (1929), where there was an attempt by town assessors to quash a writ of certiorari to review their assessment of property, on the ground that the relator had wilfully refused to answer certain questions, it was held that the proof failed to show wilful refusal, and that any defect in relator's procedure in filling out a tax questionnaire had been waived by the assessors. In the course of the opinion upon these topics the court said, in a dictum as to the rules of evidence: "Proceedings before taxing boards are not governed by the rules of practice prevailing in civil actions, and minor irregularities and informalities do not vitiate them. On such hearings the rigid rules of evidence do not apply. The assessors may take unsworn statements of an agent or attorney. People *ex rel.* Empire Mortgage Co. *v.* Cantor, 190 App. Div. 512, 180 N. Y. S. 139; People *ex rel.* Haile *v.* Brundage, 195 App. Div. 745, 187 N. Y. S. 460. In discussing this subject in the case last cited, Mr. Justice Van Kirk, then sitting at Special Term and whose opinion was adopted by the Appellate Division, said: 'The assessors, in seeking information and determining the amount of an assessment, are not limited to the rules of evidence prevailing in courts; they acquire information from observation, from hearsay, from inquiries and from the opinion of others.'"

[164] Lowell *v.* Commissioners of Middlesex County, IV D *supra*.

[165] Western Union Tel. Co. *v.* Dodge County; People *ex rel.* Schabacker *v.* State Assessors; and People *ex rel.* Hunt *v.* Priest, all IV D *supra*.

[166] People *ex rel.* Empire Mortgage Co. *v.* Cantor, and People *ex rel.* American Mfg. Co. *v.* Gifford, both IV D *supra*.

CHAP. IV]   THE RULES OF EVIDENCE   51

fruitless."[167] The rules of evidence infringed are the hearsay rule,[168] the rule forbidding opinions,[169] and the rule that testimony is to be under oath.[170] The evidentiary materials held admissible in violation of the rules include former tax abatement returns,[171] former judicial determinations,[172] evidence taken secretly from presumably prejudiced witnesses,[173] commercial ratings,[174] investors' manuals,[175] carriers' reports,[176] statements of consideration in deeds,[177] and affidavits.[178] In these cases are to be found but one expression of limitation upon the freedom of the tribunals with the rules of evidence, that there must not be arbitrary action, evidence essential to the protection of either party must be received.[179] The limitation expressed in *Lowell* v. *Commissioners of Middlesex County*,[180] that the commission must not use wrong standards of value, is a substantive, not an adjective requirement.

E. *Alien Exclusion and Deportation Hearings.*[181] For convenience

[167] People v. Hicks, IV D *supra*.
[168] Pratt v. Raymond; Western Union Tel. Co. v. Dodge County; People v. Hicks; People *ex rel.* Schabacker v. State Assessors; People *ex rel.* Hunt v. Priest, all IV D *supra*.
[169] Lowell v. Commissioners of Middlesex County, IV D *supra*.
[170] People *ex rel.* Empire Mortgage Co. v. Cantor; Pratt v. Raymond, both IV D *supra*.
[171] Lowell v. Commissioners of Middlesex County, IV D *supra*.
[172] Lake Co. v. Laconia, IV D *supra*.
[173] Pratt v. Raymond, IV D *supra*.
[174] *Ibid*.
[175] Western Union Tel. Co. v. Dodge County, IV D *supra*.
[176] People v. Hicks, IV D *supra*.
[177] People *ex rel.* Schabacker v. State Assessors, IV D *supra*.
[178] People *ex rel.* Hunt v. Priest, IV D *supra*.
[179] People *ex rel.* Schabacker v. State Assessors, IV D *supra*.
[180] IV D *supra*.
[181] Understanding of the cases relating to aliens will be aided by an explanation of the statutes and procedure involved, and the type of hearings held in connection with the control of aliens under the laws of the United States. The statutes are as follows: (The following resumé of deportation statutes and procedure thereunder is in large part based upon the *Administration of the Deportation Laws of the United States, a Report to the National Commission on Law Observance and Enforcement*, by Reuben Oppenheimer, in Volume 2, parts 5–8, National Commission on Law Observance and Enforcement (1931). Credit for the resumé, both for substance thereof, and to some extent for phrasing, is extended. Reference to the following statutes may also be made: Respecting exclusion at time of entry and aliens excluded, 8 U. S. C. §§ 136, 137, and 212. Respecting method of exclusion, 8 U. S. C. §§ 150 and 147. Respecting deportation after entry and classes subject to deportation,

in discussion the judicial decisions concerning the rules of evidence in deportation and exclusion hearings have been classified according to the rule of evidence infringed.

8 U. S. C. §§ 153, 155, 156, 157, and 137. Respecting procedure for deportation, 8 U. S. C. § 155. Respecting criminal penalties, 8 U. S. C. §§ 180–180d. With respect to Chinese exclusion, 8 U. S. C. §§ 261–299.)

The Immigration Law of 1882, the first act, provided only for deportation of aliens excluded at ports of entry. In 1888 provision was made for deportation, within a time limit, of contract laborers entering in violation of law. The first general system for expulsion and deportation of aliens after landing was provided for in the Act of 1891. The Act of 1917, a general immigration act, enlarged the provisions concerning expulsion, and this act with subsequent amendments is the present basis of what are called "warrant proceedings," hereinafter explained. The Act of 1917 provides that aliens found to be unlawfully in this country "shall upon the warrant of the Secretary of Labor be taken into custody and deported. . . ." The Chinese exclusion laws provide for removal to the country whence the alien came, after being brought before some justice, judge, or commissioner of a United States court, and found by him not lawfully entitled to remain in the United States. The expulsion of certain Chinese unlawfully living here, but not coming within general deportation provisions, is still under the jurisdiction of the federal courts, although most Chinese cases are handled administratively as warrant proceedings.

The statutes differentiate between aliens deportable because of manner of entry, or condition or status at entry, and aliens deportable because of their condition or action after entry. The former class includes, for example: paupers, diseased persons, mental or physical defectives, criminals, polygamists, and persons likely to become a public charge; also aliens who prior to entry have been convicted of or admit a felony or other crime involving moral turpitude, aliens entering at a non-designated time or place, or without inspection, or by false representations. In the second class are included anarchists or aliens advising, teaching, or members of, or affiliated with, any organization, advising or teaching opposition to organized government, or believing in or teaching the overthrow by force or violence of the United States Government; also aliens who within five years after entry become public charges from causes not affirmatively shown to have arisen after landing; aliens convicted within five years after entry of a crime involving moral turpitude and sentenced to imprisonment for one year or more, or sentenced more than once to such a term for a crime involving moral turpitude committed at any time after entry; aliens importing aliens for the purpose of prostitution, or convicted of violation of the Narcotic Act, or interned under war legislation, or convicted under war or foreign-relations legislation. There are various time limits under the Act of 1917 and its amendments, within which the various classes of aliens are deportable. The legal effect of deportation is permanent exile under the Act of March 4, 1929. There are certain criminal penalties for entering or attempting to enter after deportation, and for entering at any time or place other than as designated by immigration officials, and for eluding inspection and obtaining entry by false representations.

Under the foregoing laws, the procedure is as follows: Except for certain

CHAP. IV] THE RULES OF EVIDENCE 53

1. *Statement of General Rule.* Mr. Justice Brandeis in *United*

Chinese whose expulsion, as above stated, can only be by court proceeding, the Secretary of Labor has sole authority to deport aliens. There is no statutory provision for general judicial review. Such review as is possible in the courts is by writ of habeas corpus. The United States has been divided into thirty-five districts, each of which is under the jurisdiction of a commissioner of immigration and in each of which there are a number of inspectors. The latter investigate aliens supposed to be unlawfully in the United States and make, as the first step towards deportation, what is known as a "preliminary examination," which consists of an oral examination of the suspect covering the time and manner of his entry, and such other matters as the inspector may regard as pertinent under the deportation and exclusion statutes. Upon the basis of this preliminary examination, the inspector applies to the Secretary of Labor in Washington for a warrant of arrest which, under the rules of the department, is supposed to be issued only when the application states facts showing prima facie that the alien is subject to deportation. Upon issuance and service of the warrant of arrest charging in general terms violation of the Immigration Law, the alien is detained pending hearing, unless he furnishes bond or is released upon his own recognizance, being kept in detention quarters or jail. Thereafter there is a "warrant hearing" at which the alien is given opportunity to show cause why he should not be deported. This hearing is before an immigration inspector, often the same one who conducted the preliminary examination. Usually the government's case at the hearing is the record of the preliminary examination, but other evidence may be offered, and the alien is entitled at this hearing to inspect the warrant of arrest and to be represented by counsel. A record of the testimony is made at this hearing. After this hearing the record is sent to the Department of Labor in Washington, with the recommendation of the inspector for deportation, or cancellation of warrant, and with the record is sent all the data in the case. The record is reviewed by a non-statutory body in the Department of Labor called the board of review, appointed by the Secretary of Labor. Hearings may be had before this board upon request, but as a matter of general practice the record is reviewed in private and the board of review then makes written recommendations to the Secretary of Labor. The record, with these recommendations, is then passed upon by an assistant to the Secretary of Labor, or an Assistant Secretary, who finally decides whether a deportation warrant should be issued.

Prior to 1917 the warrant hearings were before a single official, but the Act of 1917 provided for the appointment by the commissioner of immigration, or by the inspector in charge at the various ports of arrival, of such "boards of special inquiry" as may be necessary for the prompt determination of all cases of immigrants detained at such ports, each board to consist of three members selected from such immigrant officials as have by the Commissioner General of Immigration, with the approval of the Secretary of Labor, been designated as qualified to serve. These boards have authority to determine whether an alien shall be allowed to land or shall be deported. Their hearings are not public, but the immigrant may have one friend or relative present. These boards keep a permanent record of their proceedings and the testimony

States ex rel. Bilokumsky v. *Tod* [182] has stated the general rule for all the cases as follows: [183] "Moreover, a hearing granted does not cease to be fair, merely because rules of evidence and of procedure applicable in judicial proceedings have not been strictly followed by the executive; or because some evidence has been improperly rejected or received.[184] To render a hearing unfair the defect, or the practice complained of, must have been such as might have led to a denial of justice, or there must have been absent one of the elements deemed essential to due process."[185] In the case in which Mr. Justice Brandeis thus spoke, an alleged alien, in habeas corpus, was questioned while detained in jail pending the warrant hearing, and admitted his alienage. At the hearing, upon the charge of having in his possession for distribution printed matter advocating overthrow of the government by force or violence, he refused to testify, and the report of his examination in jail was introduced in evidence to prove his alienage. He was ordered deported and sought release in habeas corpus proceedings, and therein, from an order of the District Court of the United States for New York remanding him to custody for deportation, he appealed on the ground that there was no legal evidence of alienage, a jurisdictional fact. It was held that the examination in jail was admissible. Mr. Justice Brandeis further stated: [186] "So far as appears, there was nothing in the circumstances under which Bilokumsky was examined which would have rendered his answer inadmissible even in a criminal case. The mere fact that it was given while he was in confinement would not make it so. And since deportation proceedings are in their nature civil, the rule excluding involuntary confessions could have no application."[187] The case thus is a dictum so far as the right of an administrative tribunal not to apply the rules of evidence is concerned because, as stated by Mr. Justice

taken. The decision of any two members prevails and is final, except that the alien or any dissenting member may appeal through the commissioner of immigration at the port of arrival and the Commissioner General of Immigration to the Secretary of Labor. (See 8 U. S. C. § 153.)

[182] 263 U. S. 149 (1923).
[183] *Idem* 157.
[184] Citing Tang Tun v. Edsell, 223 U. S. 673, 681.
[185] Citing Chin Yow v. United States, 208 U. S. 8, and Kwock Jan Fat v. White, 253 U. S. 454, 459.
Compare Interstate Commerce Commission v. Louisville & N. R. Co., IV A *supra*.
[186] 263 U. S. 149, 157.
[187] Citing Newhall v. Jenkins, 2 Gray 562, 563.

CHAP. IV]   THE RULES OF EVIDENCE   55

Brandeis, the statement here involved would have been admissible even in a criminal case; but, like the dictum in *Interstate Commerce Commission* v. *Baird*,[188] referred to in connection with the Interstate Commerce Commission cases, it is often quoted, and the case itself is often referred to, as authority for the rule governing the admission or rejection of evidence in these alien hearings.

2. *Impeachment.* In *Moy Said Ching* v. *Tillinghast*,[189] the issue in a warrant proceeding [190] was whether the applicant was the natural or the adopted son of a Chinese. If the latter, he was subject to deportation. At the hearing the alleged father testified that the applicant was his natural son. On three different occasions prior thereto he had testified before immigration authorities that the applicant was adopted, this as a result of advice that only an adopted son could enter. The immigration records containing these statements were received in evidence, not only to contradict the testimony of the alleged father, but as affirmative proof that the applicant was not his natural son, and an order of exclusion was made. In habeas corpus proceedings reaching the Circuit Court of Appeals, it was contended that the order was not supported by affirmative evidence. The court held otherwise, saying: "As said by this court . . .[191] 'The officials before whom the hearings were had were not restricted in the reception of evidence to only such as would meet the requirements of legal proof, but could receive and determine the questions before them upon any evidence that seemed to them worthy of credit.' The common-law rule that such statements can only be used to contradict the different version of the witness given on the stand and not as affirmative of the facts stated [192] is not applicable to hearings before immigration authorities; for, as above stated, they are entitled to 'receive and determine the questions before them upon any evidence that [seems] to them worthy of credit.'"[193] It was held, therefore, that the evidence was properly received and constituted affirmative proof upon the point at issue.[194]

[188] IV A *supra*.
[189] 21 F. (2d) 810 (C. C. A. 1st, 1927).
[190] Apparently before a board of special inquiry.
[191] Citing Johnson v. Kock Shing, 3 F. (2d) 889.
[192] Citing Lydston v. Rockingham County Light & Power Co., 75 N. H. 23, 25, 70 A. 385, 21 Ann. Cas. 1236.
[193] 21 F. (2d) 810, 811.
[194] In Jung See v. Nash, 4 F. (2d) 639 (C. C. A. 8th, 1925), it was held that it was not improper to introduce into the record sent to the Commissioner

3. *Conclusions.* In *Brader* v. *Zurbrick*,[195] a woman claimed citizenship by marriage to one who himself claimed citizenship under the naturalization of his father. At a warrant hearing testimony of the husband was admitted, to the effect that his father voted in elections, had naturalization papers, was naturalized in a named city and state, all before the witness reached majority. The government attempted to meet this by an unverified statement contained in a letter from the clerk of the superior court at the city and state named, to the effect that the court records failed to show naturalization papers issued to the witness or his father. The woman was ordered deported to Germany as a prostitute, and by habeas corpus attacked the order of deportation on the ground that the government had failed to establish the fact of alienage or the fact of her being a prostitute. It was held that the evidence of naturalization, while not the best evidence, was enough to shift the duty of going forward with evidence to the contrary.[196] A discharge was ordered for failure of the government to prove alienage.

4. *Evidence Immaterial because Not Connected.* In *United States* v. *Hughes*,[197] there was admitted at a warrant hearing upon a charge of entering contrary to law, exhaustion of quota, likelihood of becoming a public charge, and entering at a point not designated a port of entry, an alleged statement of the alien before a Texas immigration inspector to the effect that the alien was a native of Italy and smuggled into the United States from Mexico. The exhibit, written in English, was shown to the alien, who waived reading and interpreting, but admitted that the statements alleged to have been made before the Texas inspector were true. In habeas corpus proceedings, it was the contention of the applicant that the statement thus introduced at the hearing was not identified as the one made before the inspector in Texas and, hence, that there was no valid evidence to support the deportation order; that full and fair hearing means in every sense a trial in which the

General, contradictory statements of a witness in another proceeding, for the purpose of impeaching his testimony, without confronting the witness or the alien therewith.

[195] 38 F. (2d) 472 (C. C. A. 6th, 1930).

[196] Curiously, this sanction of the admission in evidence of the witness' legal conclusion that his father was naturalized was accompanied in the same decision by a ruling excluding the letter of the clerk as to the contents of the court records.

[197] 299 Fed. 99 (C. C. A. 3d, 1924).

rules of evidence applicable at trials must be invoked to assure him due process of law. It was held that the hearing was not unfair as being without evidence. The court said:[198] " . . . In ascertaining whether there is or is not any proof tending to sustain a charge involved in a case like this, it is not open to courts to consider either admissibility or weight of proof according to the ordinary rules of evidence,[199] even if the court believes the proof was insufficient and the conclusion wrong. . . ." In a court of law it would have been necessary to identify the statement, to prove that the offered statement was in fact the one which it purported on its face to be; that is, the Texas inspector must have been called to identify the exhibit unless the applicant could and did himself identify it.

5. *Former Conviction.* In *United States ex rel. Tomasso* v. *Flynn*,[200] the charge was that of being connected with a house of prostitution, and sharing benefit from the earnings of a prostitute. The evidence at a warrant hearing included the duly certified record of conviction of the alien in a county court for keeping a disorderly house. He contended in a habeas corpus proceeding that the record of his conviction should not have been admitted. The court held to the contrary, saying:[201] "It is well settled that in deportation proceedings the rules of evidence need not be followed with the same strictness as in the courts."[202] In judicial proceedings a record of conviction would not have been admitted as proof of the substance of the charge,[203] since the former trial was between different parties and a legally different cause.[204]

6. *Denial of Cross-Examination.* In *Chin Ah Yoke* v. *White*,[205]

---

[198] 299 Fed. 99, 101.

[199] Citing Lee Lung v. Patterson, 186 U. S. 168, 176, 22 Sup. Ct. 795, 46 L. ed. 1108.

[200] 22 F. (2d) 174 (Dist. Ct. N. Y. 1927).

[201] *Idem*, 176.

[202] It was also held proper to admit in this case a certified copy of the record of the county court proceedings, including certified copies of affidavits as to the character of the house in question. Affiants were not produced and the alien had no opportunity to cross-examine them. The holding in respect of cross-examination was, however, in part based upon waiver.

[203] Jones, *Evidence* (2d ed., 1908) § 589, 1 Wigmore, *Evidence* (2d ed., 1923) § 194, pp. 417, 418.

[204] In Caranica v. Nagle, 23 F. (2d) 545 (C. C. A. 9th, 1928) the admission in a warrant hearing of an inspector's testimony that the alien had been convicted under another name for violation of the National Prohibition Act was held not improper. It was shown after the admission of this testimony that it was untrue. [205] 244 Fed. 940 (C. C. A. 9th, 1917).

the alien was ordered deported as being a Chinese prostitute. The evidence at the warrant hearing consisted of the testimony, taken at a preliminary hearing in one state, of a citizen who returned to another. The alien contended that the warrant hearing was unfair for lack of opportunity to cross-examine this witness. The officers had offered to allow cross-examination if the alien had the means to return the witness. It was held that this was all that they were required to do, or could do, and that the hearing was not unfair.[206]

7. *Testimony of Wife against Husband.* In *Cahan* v. *Carr*,[207] an alien was ordered deported upon the ground that he had entered the United States without inspection and not in possession of an unexpired immigration visa. His wife testified that he admitted to her in a telephone conversation that he had visited Mexico on or about the date of entry alleged. In habeas corpus proceedings testing the fairness of a warrant hearing it was held that the admission of the wife's testimony was not error. "With certain ex-

[206] In Caranica v. Nagle, *supra*, the court sanctioned testimony by an inspector to statements made by a third party not subpoenaed, and whom the alien was given no opportunity to cross-examine, this upon the ground that the statements afforded little information upon the issues and that, even if conceded to have been incompetent, they were not ground for reversal because not relied upon or mentioned in the summary which the board of review submitted to the Secretary of Labor. It is thus assumed that administrative officials are better able than jurors or judges to disregard incompetent testimony. The same case holds that the fact that an inspector testified to hearsay statements that an alien was a Greek procurer and had a wife practicing prostitution, and that upon cross-examination he refused to disclose the names of his informants, did not show that the hearing was unfair.

But contrast with these cases Whitfield v. Hanges, 222 Fed. 745 (C. C. A. 9th, 1915), forbidding denial of cross-examination and deportation upon hearsay and gravely prejudicial rumor of which the aliens had no notice and which they had no opportunity to refute. Whitfield v. Hanges was an aggravated case of unfair action by an immigration inspector, and indicates that there are some limits to which the warrant hearings cannot be carried with judicial sanction. The aliens were not allowed in that case to participate in the hearing, and upon the faith of Interstate Commerce Commission v. Baird, IV A *supra*, it was held that there was no hearing in the legal sense.

See also: Kwock Jan Fat v. White, 253 U. S. 454 (1920), where failure by an inspector to place in the record an item of evidence favorable to the alien was held to render the hearing unfair, but the suppression of the names of witnesses whose statements were put in the record was held not necessarily to render it unfair.

[207] 47 F. (2d) 604 (C. C. A. 9th, 1931), *aff'g.* Ex Parte Cahan, 42 F. (2d) 664.

ceptions not material here," said the Circuit Court of Appeals, "a wife, on grounds of public policy, is not permitted to testify against her husband [208] and we perceive no good reason why the same rule of public policy should not exclude her testimony in a matter of this kind. But, be that as it may, her testimony was cumulative only, and it is well settled that the admission of incompetent testimony does not render a hearing unfair. . . ."[209]

8. *Unsworn Interpreters.* In *Lee Sim* v. *United States*,[210] at a warrant hearing before an immigration inspector, the government's interpreter was not sworn. The testimony elicited through him was material as to the place of birth of the alien, the latter claiming to have been born in the United States, and as to his having entered from Canada without inspection after six years' absence in China. It was urged in a habeas corpus proceeding that the interpreter was a witness as well as the person testifying. But the court held that it was not necessary in such hearings to put witnesses under oath; that although inspectors are empowered to administer oaths they are not required to do so; and that even if the testimony had to be given under oath it was not necessary that an official interpreter, under oath to discharge his duties faithfully, should be required to take separate oath in each case.[211]

9. *Hearsay.* (a) *Miscellaneous Cases.* In *United States* v. *Uhl*,[212] the sole question was whether there was any evidence to sustain a finding of immigration officials that the aliens in question were likely to become public charges. The immigration officials had found this as a fact and ordered them deported. The hearing was before a board of special inquiry which had ascertained by reports in the public press and other sources that, owing to depressed labor conditions, the prospect of unskilled laborers obtaining work in

[208] Citing Lucas v. Brooks, 18 Wall. 436, 453, 21 L. ed. 779.

[209] Citing Bilokumsky v. Tod, IV E 1 *supra*. The alien in Cahan v. Carr had resided in the United States since 1919 as a citizen of Canada. It was charged that he had visited Tia Juana, Mexico, on or about May 1, 1929, and returned to the United States on the same day. The court held that there was no merit to the contention that the alien was exempt from the requirement of the immigration law because of the brevity of his visit to the foreign country. Numerous authorities were cited to this effect.

[210] 218 Fed. 432 (C. C. A. 2d, 1914).

[211] There was a similar ruling in Jeung Bow v. United States, 228 Fed. 868 (C. C. A. 2d, 1915).

[212] 215 Fed. 573 (C. C. A. 2d, 1914).

Portland, Oregon, to which place the aliens were routed with meagre funds, was most unfavorable. Objections being made to the form of this evidence, the Circuit Court of Appeals said: [213] "It is true that information in this form would not be permitted in a court of law, but the immigration officers cannot delay these proceedings indefinitely. They cannot summon witnesses from the Pacific states or send commissions there. If they were satisfied from information received that there was no market in Portland for such services as these relators could render, they were justified in acting upon such information, just as they would be if satisfied from reports in the press or from any reliable source that Portland had been destroyed by flood or fire or that an epidemic of cholera was raging there. Congress has placed the determination of these questions in the hands of trained officials and their conclusions upon disputed questions of fact are final and conclusive. It is only in the very rare instance that a finding is without any proof to support it that the courts may interfere."[214] In a similar case, *Healy* v. *Backus*,[215] in which Hindoos were excluded as likely to become public charges, it was held, upon the faith of *United States* v. *Uhl*,[216] that affidavits, interviews, letters, and newspaper clippings showing the state of the public mind in California towards Hindoos as a race or class, and the condition of the labor market in general and especially as it related to Hindoos, the desirability or non-desirability among employers for their employment, and the demand or lack of demand for labor of the kind, were admissible and sufficient to warrant the findings and order of the officials; that is, that they constituted some evidence tending to support the findings.

The written statement of a father, not produced as a witness,

[213] 215 Fed. 573, 574.

[214] This case was later reversed (239 U. S. 3, 1915), but the reversal was not upon the ground that hearsay evidence was improperly admitted at the hearing, but upon the ground that, even if it were true that the state of the labor market at Portland made it likely that the aliens would become public charges, this was not a proper ground for excluding the aliens from admission, the federal statutes dealing with admission to the United States and not with admission to Portland. Mr. Justice Holmes stated that it would be an amazing claim of power if commissioners decided not to admit aliens because the labor market of the United States was overstocked. *A fortiori*, they cannot decide against the admission of aliens simply because of a local labor market being overstocked.

[215] 221 Fed. 358 (C. C. A. 9th, 1915).

[216] Just discussed.

CHAP. IV] THE RULES OF EVIDENCE 61

that he was born in China, this being material evidence against the claim of an alien that he was the foreign-born son of a native-born Chinese, was admitted in *White* v. *Chan Wy Sheung*[217] under a ruling [218] that "It is not open to the courts to consider either the admissibility or the weight of proof according to the ordinary rules of evidence, and the fact that the rules of evidence as applied in courts of law are violated does not show that the hearing was unfair. . . ." [219] In *Moy Yoke Shue* v. *Johnson*,[220] an alien claimed admission as the son of one Moy Yee Ai, who was concededly an American citizen. At the warrant hearing the immigration officials admitted the statement of one Moy San Lee in a proceeding relating to the admission of his son, with which hearing the alien in the instant case and Moy Yee Ai, his alleged father, were in no way connected. Moy San Lee had testified in 1921 that he had a brother of the same name as Moy Yee Ai and that this brother was unmarried. At the hearing in the instant case Moy Yee Ai, the alleged father, had identified a picture of Moy San Lee as being his brother and testified that they had quarrelled years before and had had nothing to do with each other since. The principal ground of objection to the fairness of the hearing was the admission of the statements of Moy San Lee in the prior proceeding. In habeas corpus the court held that the hearing was not rendered unfair and said:[221] "What the immigration tribunal did in effect was to admit against the applicant declarations relevant to the issue, made under oath by a third party, in the absence of the applicant. It is well settled that administrative tribunals are not bound by the rules of evidence which are recognized in courts of law. The test is whether, under a correct understanding of the fundamental principles of law applicable to the case, they have honestly endeavored to arrive at the truth by methods sufficiently fair and reasonable to amount to due process of law." [222]

[217] 270 Fed. 765 (C. C. A. 9th, 1921).
[218] *Idem*, 766.
[219] Healy *v.* Backus, *supra*, and other cases were cited.
[220] 290 Fed. 621 (Dist. Ct. Mass., 1923).
[221] Speaking through Mr. Justice Morton, p. 622 of 290 Fed.
[222] In this case the court was influenced by what might be called circumstantial guarantees of the verity of the third party's statement, to wit, that it was not unreasonable to believe that Moy San Lee knew whether Yee Ai was married when the two came to America together in 1901, it being without dispute that the two were intimately associated then, and that ". . . it is going a good way to assume that San Lee, when he testified in his son's case in

In *United States ex rel. Smith* v. *Curran*,[223] hearsay was introduced through hearsay. There was an application for entry by a widow and her minor son. She claimed entry as a preference quota immigrant skilled in agriculture and presented a German police identification certificate and a quota immigration visa purporting to have been issued by the United States Consul at Koenigsburg, Germany. There were several hearings before a board of special inquiry. At one of them a telegram to the Secretary of State, received from the United States Consul at Rotterdam, stating that the sender had been informed by the American Consul at Berlin that the aliens "are alleged to have forged visas purporting to be issued by the consulate at Koenigsburg," was received, and also a letter from the Assistant Chief Visa Officer of the State Department in Washington stating:[224] ". . . We have received another cablegram from the American consul at Koenigsburg, dated June 17th, specifically stating that his office did not issue visas to Mary Schulhoff and child. . . ." The court said:[225] "It is now long established, in proceedings in immigration cases, that neither the hearsay rule nor the best evidence rule, nor, indeed, any of the common-law rules of evidence, need be observed. A board of special inquiry, which determines these cases, may consider hearsay evidence and administrative findings, although based upon evidence which would not be competent in a court of law, which evidence may not be attacked upon habeas corpus. . . ."

The *ex parte* statements of "customers," of immoral relations for pay with an alien ordered deported for practicing prostitution subsequent to entry, were sanctioned in *United States ex rel. Ng Wing* v. *Brough*,[226] the same being testified to by an inspector. The court there recognized that "receiving statements of the character here received necessarily denies the opportunity of cross-examination; but the law permits, in a summary proceeding such as this, that such statements be received for what they are worth, with knowledge of the fact that there was no cross-examination. . . ."[227]

1921, foresaw that Yee Ai, nearly two years later, would attempt to bring in his son, and falsified in order to defeat Yee Ai's effort, and thereby do him injury because of the quarrel which they had had." (See p. 623 of 290 Fed.)

See also Johnson *v.* Kock Shing, 3 F. (2d) 889 (C. C. A. 1st, 1925), another case admitting the statement of a third party, and warranting the reception of "any evidence that seemed . . . worthy of credit." (See p. 889 of 3 F. [2d].)

[223] 12 F. (2d) 636 (C. C. A. 2d, 1926).   [224] *Idem*, 637.
[225] Speaking through Mr. Justice Manton, p. 637 of 12 F. (2d).
[226] 15 F. (2d) 377 (C. C. A. 2d, 1926).   [227] *Idem*, 379.

CHAP. IV]   THE RULES OF EVIDENCE   63

In this case, according to the court, there was other evidence apart from the *ex parte* testimony to support the findings.[228]

Ng Mon Tong v. *Weedin*[229] supports the reception in evidence of the certificate of a surgeon of the United States Public Health Service to the effect that, judging from the alien's general appearance, his teeth, and sexual development, he was between the ages of seventeen and twenty-two years. If the alien were appreciably older than twelve years he could not be the son of the native-born Chinese citizen of the United States claimed as his father. There was other similar testimony in the case by witnesses present but no authentic information as to age. The order of deportation was sustained.[230]

The admission of the signed statements of three prostitutes, and also the testimony of an inspector as to what they had said, was sanctioned in *Kip Wah* v. *Nagle*[231] against an alien ordered deported as employed in a house of prostitution. *United States ex rel. Bilokumsky* v. *Tod*[232] was quoted. There was evidence, apart from the admissions of the women, that the house was a house of prostitution and that the alien knew it, that he had admitted that he was employed there and that he was an alien.

At a preliminary hearing in *Chin Shee* v. *White*,[233] an immigration inspector injected into the record the following: "Alien, when arrested on the street, was loudly dressed, bedecked with jewelry, and face painted; it is common knowledge in Chinatown that she is a prostitute, though of course the Chinese, by reason of their peculiar laws among themselves, cannot make affidavit to that effect, because of fear of assassination by a Tong man."[234] This case reached the Secretary of Labor on appeal through the Immigration Bureau, and was reviewed finally in habeas corpus proceedings against the commissioner of immigration at Seattle. The Circuit Court of Appeals held that the injection of this matter into the record did not vitiate the fairness of the hear-

[228] The court also held that in this case, there being no issue of citizenship, the aliens were not entitled to a judicial hearing, even in the district court, in review of the deportation proceedings in habeas corpus.

[229] 43 F. (2d) 718 (C. C. A. 9th, 1930).

[230] Contrast, however, United States *ex rel.* Fong On *v.* Day, 39 F. (2d) 202 (Dist. Ct. N. Y. 1930).

[231] 7 F. (2d) 426 (C. C. A. 9th, 1925).

[232] IV E 1 *supra*.

[233] 273 Fed. 801 (C. C. A. 9th, 1921).

[234] *Idem*, 805.

ing or the appeal, that "... the officers of the government are not bound by strict rules of evidence applied in criminal cases in courts of justice ... and it is inconceivable that the judgment of the Secretary of Labor was controlled in any degree by the interjection of this bit of irrelevant matter."[235] There was, according to the court, however, ample evidence of a legitimate character in the record to support the finding that the alien ordered deported had been found practicing prostitution subsequent to entry.

(b) *Hearsay in the Form of Affidavits.* This is frequently admitted. Thus, in *United States* v. *Uhl*,[236] an Italian was ordered deported on the ground that he advocated unlawful destruction of property. At the hearing an affidavit was introduced wherein affiant had sworn that the Italian had told him that he and his associates would blow up the shops of certain manufacturers if a strike were not settled. In habeas corpus proceedings appealed to the United States Circuit Court of Appeals, it was urged that the hearing was not fair because of the admission of this hearsay affidavit. But it was, as usual, held that the ordinary rules of evidence do not apply to such proceedings and that the affidavit was admissible, notwithstanding that the affiant was not produced at the hearing for cross-examination. The case was in part based upon the proposition, however, that the right of cross-examination had been waived by failure to request it.

The admission in evidence of affidavits of prostitutes, in hearings charging aliens with sharing in the earnings of prostitutes and being connected with houses of prostitution as a ground for deportation, was sanctioned in *Ex Parte Garcia*,[237] *Ex Parte Mouratis*,[238] and *Ghiggeri* v. *Nagle*.[239]

(c) *Records in Other Proceedings.* The practice has been sanctioned, under the theory that the rules of evidence do not apply in administrative hearings, of introducing into the record in a given proceeding the contents of records in others. In *Tang Tun* v. *Edsell*,[240] the alien claimed to be a citizen born in Seattle of parents

[235] 273 Fed. 801, 805.
[236] 266 Fed. 34 (C. C. A. 2d, 1920).
[237] 205 Fed. 53 (Dist. Ct. Cal., 1913).
[238] 21 F. (2d) 694 (Dist. Ct. Cal., 1927).
[239] 19 F. (2d) 875 (C. C. A. 9th, 1927).

Other cases upholding the reception of affidavits are: Choy Gum *v.* Backus, 223 Fed. 487 (C. C. A. 9th, 1915) and *Ex Parte* Zavala, 298 Fed. 544 (Dist. Ct. Texas, 1924).

[240] 223 U. S. 673 (1912).

CHAP. IV] THE RULES OF EVIDENCE 65

there domiciled, that he went to China in 1884 and returned in 1897, that he was admitted by the collector of customs at that time and that in 1905 he returned to China again and married. He returned in 1906, seeking entry for himself and wife, but was refused. Included within his evidence was a purported endorsement of the collector of customs in 1897 as to the fact of admission. It was claimed, however, that he had, notwithstanding that, been rejected at that date; and upon this issue the inspector forwarded to the Secretary of Labor the papers from the official files in cases of other Chinese persons who arrived on the same steamer, some of whom had identification papers similar to those of the alien in question, with endorsement of the same collector purporting to show their admission, in conflict with the office records showing their rejection. The inspector called the attention of the Secretary to the fact that in certain cases, after inquiry before the United States Commissioner and despite the possession of such identification by the collector, deportation had been ordered. Of these official files and the contents thereof the Supreme Court of the United States said: "Of these the Secretary might at all times take cognizance, and it would be extraordinary indeed to impute bad faith or improper conduct to the executive officers because they examined the records or acquainted themselves with former official action."[241] The case holds that it is not unfair for executive officers to examine official records and acquaint themselves with former official action prejudicial to the alien, and to communicate the same to the Secretary of Labor on appeal, where the executive officer truthfully reports the contents of the records.[242] In *Chin Shee* v. *White*,[243] letters and memoranda consisting of correspondence between the immigration commissioner at Seattle and an inspector in another city, and between the Seattle commissioner and the Commissioner General at Washington, and certain statements and testimony of witnesses accompanying this correspondence taken prior to the arrest of the alien ordered deported, were included in the record certified from Washington to the Circuit Court of Appeals in habeas corpus proceedings. They were not a part of the record made at the hearing before the inspector. It was

[241] 223 U. S. 673, 681.
[242] In this case the inspector also stated to the Secretary the result of his investigation of official files disclosing facts having a material bearing upon the question of whether or not the alien was rejected in 1897.
[243] 273 Fed. 801 (C. C. A. 9th, 1921). *Cit. supra* on another point, IV E 9 (a).

held [244] that the Secretary of Labor might properly take cognizance of such correspondence and matter accompanying it; that neither bad faith nor improper conduct could be imputed to the executive officers because they examined the records or acquainted themselves with former official action.[245]

It is of interest to note that in some instances the rules of evidence are relaxed in favor of the alien rather than against him. Thus, in *United States* v. *Curran*,[246] a native of Russia sought admission to the United States from Argentina, claiming to have lived there continuously for five years immediately preceding the time of his application for admission to the United States, this entitling him to admission under a proviso excepting such aliens from the quota fixed.[247] A board of special inquiry refused to give consideration to a certificate from the alien's employer in South America, and to a La Plata court certificate, which indicated that he had lived in Argentina for more than five years. It was held that the hearing was unfair, since the evidence upon which he claimed right of admission was ignored.[248]

Reviewing the cases concerning the rules of evidence in deportation and exclusion hearings, it appears that while there must be no such defect in the proceedings as might lead to "denial of justice," and no element lacking "essential to due process,"[249] and that

[244] Tang Tun *v.* Edsell, IV E 9 (c) *supra*, was cited.

[245] In Ex Parte Jurgans, 17 F. (2d) 507 (Dist. Ct. Minn. 1927), copies of exhibits in another case were introduced for the purpose of establishing the character of an organization alleged to advocate the overthrow by force of the government.

See also Soo Hoo Do Yim *v.* Tillinghast, 24 F. (2d) 163 (C. C. A. 1st, 1928), supporting the admission of department-file records containing the testimony of a third party alleged to show discrepancies between his testimony and that of the alien, who claimed him as a brother. The alien was given opportunity to explain. It was held further that the discrepancies were not important and apparently not relied upon by the board of review, although mentioned and perhaps given consideration by the board of special inquiry.

It is possible that some of the official records allowed in evidence might come within the public-document exception to the hearsay rule, but not that part of such records which includes testimony given by third parties.

[246] 4 F. (2d) 356 (C. C. A. 3rd, 1925).

[247] By § 2 of the Act of May 19, 1921, 42 Stat. 5, c. 8, as amended by 42 Stat. 540, § 2.

[248] Contrast with the usual attitude of the courts in the hearsay cases, Lewis *ex rel.* Lai Thuey Lem *v.* Johnson, 16 F. (2d) 180 (C. C. A. 1st, 1926), overturning an exclusion order based wholly on hearsay which the applicant was given no opportunity to explain or rebut.

[249] United States *ex rel.* Bilokumsky *v.* Tod, IV E 1 *supra*.

"honest endeavor to arrive at the truth by methods amounting to due process" must be made,[250] and that there must be "some evidence" to support an order,[251] nevertheless these generous phrases open a wide field indeed within which to search for facts. Hearings are "fair" not only when the rules of evidence are "not followed with the same strictness as in courts," [252] and where "the strict rules applied in criminal cases" [253] are not followed, but "any evidence worthy of credit,"[254] and "incompetent testimony"[255] may be received, and evidence may be taken for what it is "worth,"[256] and hearings may be conducted free from "any of the common law rules" without destroying "fairness." In this class of cases — in addition to violation of the hearsay rule,[257] commonly permitted in administrative practice, and of the rules against opinions [258] and immaterial evidence [259] — the opportunity for cross-examination may be denied,[260] the rules concerning impeachment broken,[261] judgments in other proceedings [262] introduced, "other crimes" considered,[263] interpreters translate without oath[264] and wife testify against husband,[265] — and still the hearings are "fair"; and the courts do not blink at the reception of statements of "common knowledge,"[266] press reports, letters, interviews, and newspaper clippings,[267] or at the affidavits of prostitutes [268] or the statements of their "customers."[269]

[250] Moy Yoke Shue *v.* Johnson, IV E 9 (a) *supra.*
[251] United States *v.* Hughes, IV E 4 *supra.*
[252] United States *ex rel.* Tomasso *v.* Flynn, IV E 5 *supra.*
[253] Chin Shee *v.* White, IV E 9 (a) *supra.*
[254] Moy Said Ching *v.* Tillinghast, IV E 2 *supra,* and Johnson *v.* Kock Shing, IV E 9 (a) *supra.* [255] Cahan *v.* Carr, IV E 7 *supra.*
[256] United States *ex rel.* Ng Wing *v.* Brough, IV E 9 (a) *supra.*
[257] See the numerous cases cited under the sub-heading "Hearsay," IV E 9 *supra.* [258] Brader *v.* Zurbrick, IV E 3 *supra.*
[259] United States *v.* Hughes, IV E 4 *supra.*
[260] Chin Ah Yoke *v.* White, IV E 6 *supra.*
[261] Moy Said Ching *v.* Tillinghast; Jung See *v.* Nash; both IV E 2 *supra.*
[262] United States *ex rel.* Tomasso *v.* Flynn, IV E 5 *supra.*
[263] Caranica *v.* Nagle, IV E 6 *supra.*
[264] Lee Sim *v.* United States, IV E 8 *supra.*
[265] Cahan *v.* Carr, IV E 7 *supra.*
[266] Chin Shee *v.* White, IV E 9 (a) *supra.*
[267] United States *v.* Uhl; Healy *v.* Backus; both IV E 9 (a) *supra.*
[268] Ex Parte Garcia; Ex Parte Mouratis; Ghiggeri *v.* Nagle; all IV E 9 (b) *supra.* [269] United States *ex rel.* Ng Wing *v.* Brough, IV E 9 (a) *supra.*

CHAPTER V

THE PRACTICE IN THE COMMISSIONS: QUESTIONNAIRE

A LETTER was sent to the chairman of the public service commission of each state in the United States, except Delaware, which has no commission, and to the Chairman of the Public Service Commission of the District of Columbia, of the Territory of Hawaii, and of Porto Rico; also to the Chairman of the Interstate Commerce Commission, of the Federal Trade Commission, and to the Commissioner General of Immigration, stating the need of information as to the actual practice in the commissions with respect to applying the rules of evidence, and as to the views of the commissioners upon the desirability of applying the rules of evidence in the commission practice. Each letter was accompanied by a questionnaire asking for answers to the questions: (1) Do you apply the rules of evidence? (2) If you apply certain of the rules and omit to apply others, please state which and why? (3) To what extent, if any, have you found in your experience that omission to apply the rules of evidence operates against obtaining an accurate understanding of the facts; and (4) To what extent, if any, have you found in your experience that applying the rules of evidence operates against obtaining an accurate understanding of the facts? Replies to the questionnaire were received from Arizona, Arkansas, Colorado, Connecticut, District of Columbia, Georgia, Territory of Hawaii, Illinois, Indiana, Iowa, Louisiana, Maine, Maryland, Massachusetts, Minnesota, Missouri, Nebraska, Nevada, New Jersey, New Mexico, New York,[1] North Carolina, Ohio, Oklahoma, Pennsylvania, Rhode Island, South Carolina, Tennessee, Texas, Utah, Vermont, Virginia, Washington, West Virginia and Wyoming; also from the Interstate Commerce Commission, and the Federal Trade Commission.

There follows a resumé of the answer from each commission replying: In *Arizona*, while the rules of evidence are not strictly adhered to, they are followed as closely "as common practice will permit." The principal departure is in the admission of secondary

[1] The Public Service Commission and the Transit Commission each replied.

CHAP. V]   THE RULES OF EVIDENCE   69

or hearsay evidence. It is not often found that this operates against obtaining an accurate understanding of the facts; and the application of the rules does "not at all" operate against obtaining an accurate understanding of the facts. The Arizona commission's "decisions are based almost wholly upon the evidence which comes under the rules." In *Arkansas* the commission does not apply the rules of evidence. "Any evidence introduced in any case before the Commission is accepted for what it may be worth. A more full and complete understanding of a case is had by not following strictly the rules of evidence." In *Colorado*, where the statute [2] provides that "neither the commission nor any commissioner shall be bound by the technical rules of evidence," the commission "does not make a practice of following strict rules of evidence which apply in courts of law." The hearsay rule is applied "when it appears that a failure to follow the rule might seriously affect the rights of the party who is objecting to the hearsay testimony." It is the experience of the commission "that the failure to follow many of the rules of evidence does not prevent the Commission from attaining an accurate understanding of the facts," and that "following said rules would in many cases prevent our obtaining such an understanding, although the extent of such prevention cannot be stated." The chairman of this commission was for many years engaged in active court practice, in both Illinois and Colorado. In *Connecticut* the rules of evidence are not applied "excepting that the evidence submitted must apply to the subject matter." The commission believes "that the informal presentation of evidence operates in favor of accurate understanding of all the facts . . . expedites the hearing and gives the Commission a fuller knowledge of all the facts, than if hedged in by technical rules of evidence." [3]

In the *District of Columbia* ". . . few, if any, of the rules are followed strictly. The commission does, however, endeavor to limit cross-examination to the scope of the direct examination. It is very liberal in its application of the hearsay rule. In the opinion of the commission its failure to apply the rules of evidence strictly does not operate against obtaining an accurate understanding of the facts." On the contrary, the commission ". . . seeks to bring out the facts and is of the opinion that its method of pro-

[2] II C *supra*.

[3] The Connecticut statutes contain no provision relating to application of the rules of evidence. II C *supra*.

cedure more nearly accomplishes its purpose than would be the result of such strict application of the rules of evidence. The rigid application of the hearsay rule would make it very difficult and expensive to obtain adequate data."

In *Georgia*[4] the Commission does "not observe judicial procedure in any sense, as observed in Georgia. Perhaps ninety per cent of the cases handled by our Commission are results of our own action, without complaint, and those cases that are heard by us on complaint are seldom represented by an attorney. Accordingly, we cannot observe any of the requirements of rules of evidence and judicial procedure. Illustrative: We permit one to read from a newspaper, give hearsay testimony and look to files in our office that are not introduced or referred to at the hearing. We find it works for economy of time to allow such a [5] relevant testimony, and on the question being asked about what controls our hearings, the answer is made that our practice works for economy of time and, of course, we pay no attention to much that is offered in the way of so-called evidence; but compared to legal observations and discussions as to the admissibility of evidence, we are convinced that we get along much better under our practice. We really have to be less observant of legal procedure than you will find even in a country justice's court." The chairman answering for the commission further states: "Having practiced law for sixteen years and having served on this Commission for the past twenty years, I am definitely fixed in the opinion that sooner or later our rules of evidence, pleading and various useless technical requirements in our judicial procedure will be done away with."

The Public Utilities Commission of the *Territory of Hawaii* responds that ". . . as a general rule" the rules of evidence are applied. "However the Commission attempts to allow any one present at a hearing to present any pertinent matter, even though involving hearsay, but requires proper evidence if any such evidence is material. The parties themselves, (i. e. the utilities) are usually represented by counsel, and as to them the rules are pretty closely followed. With regard to consumers, usually present only in person, they are frequently allowed to give both hearsay and opinion unless a representative of the utility objects. Those present are also allowed, within bounds, to interrogate parties as witnesses.

[4] Despite the statute providing that the rules of evidence shall be the same as in civil actions. II C *supra*.

[5] Undoubtedly a misprint in the letter.

The Commission does not wish to be strictly formal." In answer to the question, "To what extent, if any, omission to apply the rules of evidence has been found to operate against obtaining an accurate understanding of the facts," the Commission replies: "Not at all. Matters of hearsay and opinion, if pertinent to any issue involved are always supplemented and checked by legal evidence, and in such cases the latter controls. And any decision is based only on legal evidence. We always endeavor to have a record that will pass muster in the Appellate Court." But the Commission also has "not at all" found that applying the rules of evidence operates against obtaining an accurate understanding of the facts. "If an insistence upon legal evidence precludes all the necessary or essential facts from coming out, the Commission will secure such facts from qualified sources, and by its own initiative, if necessary, sometimes postponing a hearing for that purpose." Supplementing the foregoing answers, the reply for the Commission further states: ". . . our Commission has found it necessary to have comparatively few formal hearings. In view of the fact that most of our utilities are comparatively small the Commission has been able to adjust most matters coming before it by getting all the parties together where necessary and ironing out their troubles in an informal way. If such a procedure is not satisfactory to all concerned and if there is likely to be any question as to the Commission's findings, of course a formal hearing is had. Naturally in a case involving the establishment of a rate basis the above procedure is not followed, and the Commission in such cases proceeds fairly closely according to the established rules of evidence. . . . Our Commission has made it a policy, especially where formal hearings are had, to have the attorney for the Commission conduct the proceedings, the Commissioners of course asking such questions as they may deem necessary either through their attorney or directly. This seems rather necessary in order that the record, including the transcript, may be in proper shape for the consideration of our Supreme Court, which is the court of appeals from the Commission."

The commissioner replying for the *Illinois* Commerce Commission states: "We do not strictly adhere to the rules of evidence, and our act specifically provides that it shall not be necessary.[6] We endeavor in a general way to apply the rules of evidence, but allow a considerable latitude wherever deviation from the rules

[6] See the description of the Illinois statute. II C *supra*.

of evidence might possibly develop some facts which would be helpful to the Commission in giving consideration to the case, and which could not be admitted under a strict application of the rules of evidence. The cases are comparatively few where omission to apply the rules of evidence operates against obtaining an accurate understanding of the facts, but in view of the fact that utility regulation is comparatively a new field of legal endeavor, and the courts differ concerning the matter as to what extent a regulatory body should have jurisdiction over both the activities and records of holding companies, etc., there are cases where a deviation from the application of the rules of evidence seems helpful." But the commissioner does ". . . not wish to convey the impression . . . that we . . ." ignore ". . . the rules of evidence for the reason that, in so far as it seems practicable and does not preclude the offering of testimony to assist us in our investigations, we do quite generally adhere to the rules of evidence."

The *Indiana* commission responds that the rules of evidence are applied in part.[7] It states: "You know this body is no court — it largely depends on what the presiding commissioner wants. This is a fact finding body. Get what we want if possible." The commission does not find that omission to apply the rules impedes getting at the facts, and states further that "strict rules of evidence in matters of this kind work disadvantageously." In *Iowa* the rules are applied "but not strictly, as in courts." The essential rules "are generally observed," but there is "a very liberal hearing and construction of the rules of evidence." The *Louisiana* commission reports that the rules of evidence are applied "only to the extent that hearsay and immaterial and irrelevant testimony is excluded. . . . It is the judgment of the commission that administrative and investigative bodies, only quasi-judicial in their functions, should not apply the rigorous rules of evidence applied in courts of law." The commission has found that omission to apply the rules of evidence does not operate against obtaining an accurate understanding of the facts.[8] In *Maine* the rules of evidence are applied "but with considerable liberality." [9] The com-

[7] The Indiana statutes are silent respecting the rules of evidence. II C *supra*.

[8] The Louisiana statutes are silent respecting the rules of evidence. II C *supra*.

[9] Note the Maine statute, quoted in II C *supra*, providing that the ". . . rules of evidence shall be the same as in civil actions in the superior court. . . ."

mission chairman further states: "I think it is not always wise to be too strict in admitting evidence and except as objections are insisted upon we do not usually require strict compliance. Better results may often be thus obtained, particularly where one side or the other of a controversy is not represented by counsel or where counsel on one side or the other is unfamiliar with P. U. practice and procedure."

In *Maryland*[10] "it is the belief of the Public Service Commission . . . in the light of its own experience, that failure to apply the technical rules of evidence does not operate against obtaining an accurate understanding of the facts. On the contrary, the Commission believes that its procedure enables it to develop a more complete record than would be possible if it were strictly to adhere to the technical rules of evidence." In *Massachusetts* the commission applies the rules of evidence "to a large extent . . . but by no means strictly. . . . The main purpose of rules of evidence . . . is to expedite the proceedings. Very often the enforcing of rules of evidence would protract instead of shortening the hearing.[11] The question [12] must be decided as judgment dictates in each instance. . . . Our hearings are conducted largely in the same manner as legislative hearings." Omission to apply the rules does not operate against obtaining an accurate understanding of the facts.[13] In *Minnesota* the Railroad & Warehouse Commission does not apply the rules of evidence "with the same technical application as is observed in courts. We require an orderly proceeding but permit any answer to any question that may throw light upon the subject before the Commission." The Commission believes that this practice "enables the Commission to obtain a more accurate understanding of the facts of any matter before the Commission."

Following are the views of the chairman of the *Missouri* Public Service Commission: "I believe it would not be advisable to apply the rules of evidence to Commission practice to the same extent that they are applied to judicial proceedings. I look upon the Commission as a fact-finding body. The Commission and its staff are

[10] Where the statute, II C *supra*, provides that the commission "shall not be bound by the technical rules of evidence."
[11] This seems inconsistent with the next previous statement.
[12] Of applying the rules.
[13] The Massachusetts statutes are silent concerning the rules of evidence. II C *supra*.

composed of experts in the field in which the investigation is being made. They are, therefore, able to determine the value of evidence without being circumscribed by the rules of evidence applicable in a court. One reason for the rules of evidence in a case at law is to prevent the jury, which is not skilled in weighing evidence, from being swayed by matters not connected with the issue or by evidence of so little weight that the law excludes it. The Commission with its experts, however, is able to determine what evidence is credible, to reject evidence incompetent or evidence, from its nature, not of sufficient weight or value to be worth consideration. For example, there is no reason why the hearsay rule should be enforced as in a court of law. You do not permit hearsay evidence in a trial at law because the jury might give credence to gossip or weight to evidence which, from its nature, generally does not carry with it the stamp of credibility, and which denies the adverse party the right of cross-examination. The Commission, however, is able to weigh hearsay evidence and give it the degree of credibility to which it is entitled, and in some cases, so far as the Commission's purpose is concerned, hearsay evidence is valuable evidence. Similarly, I see no reason why the Commission should insist on the best evidence rule. If the Commission is convinced that a copy is correct it should accept it without insisting that the original or a certified copy be submitted. Another objection to applying the rules of evidence in Commission practice is that parties often appear in their own behalf and frequently cases are tried by laymen who represent their communities. In such cases, and for that matter, in all cases, the Commission is not a mere umpire between adversaries. It represents the public generally; it can and does investigate and put in evidence, through its own staff, without consideration of the parties formally before it." The chairman then refers to the Missouri statute [14] providing that the Commission "shall not be bound by the technical rules of evidence," and thereafter states: "The Public Service Commission exercises legislative powers and is a branch of the legislative power of the state. As such, I see no reason why it should not operate as a legislative committee. It should receive all credible evidence pertinent to the issue under investigation, and then make its findings upon all of the evidence submitted to it, according to its weight. Furthermore, the Commission differs from a court in that its decision is not final. The decree or judgment of a court is final

[14] II C *supra*.

CHAP. V]   THE RULES OF EVIDENCE   75

and binding upon the parties forever afterwards upon the issues presented. On the other hand, the findings and orders of the Commission are not final, even in another proceeding between the same parties where the same or similar issues are presented. It is, therefore, necessary that in a court of law the evidence presented be governed by rules somewhat inflexible. Because of the final nature of [the] transaction, a guard should be placed about the evidence presented so that the possibility of an erroneous finding of facts be eliminated so far as possible. On the other hand, the findings of a Commission, not being forever final and binding upon the parties, need not be so hedged by inflexible rules."

In *Nebraska* "about the only time we apply the strict rules of evidence, is where two or more railroads or other corporations over which we have control, are having hearings and are represented by their attorneys, then we use the same rules as are used here in District Court practice." The commission apparently, however, differentiates between cases involving service, or "the effect that certain operations might have in case the applications or complaints are acted upon favorably," and other cases. In the former, where the hearings are "inquisitory," conclusions of witnesses are called for. But the commission does "not take hearsay testimony, however, in any instance," and the rules of evidence are applied "in so far as direct testimony and exhibits are concerned."

In *Nevada* the rules of evidence are applied "generally but not literally as in a court of law. We are liberal in taking testimony, even if not in accord with court rule. Such omission or variation in rules of evidence expedites hearings and does not prevent clear understanding of facts." The commission, however, does "not recall any case . . . in which literal application of any rule may have operated against obtaining an accurate understanding of the facts."

In *New Jersey* "the strict rules of evidence are not followed. . . . It has been found by experience that with the non-application of the strict rules of evidence greater latitude is given in the production of testimony and [this] develops a broader and more accurate understanding of the facts. If strict rules of evidence were applied, such as are in force in the Courts, the record of hearings would be limited and not serve the general purpose for which the Board was created." The Board states further, however, "generally the rules of evidence are followed in the conduct of public hearings, since the Board is largely quasi judicial."

In *New Mexico* the State Corporation Commission applies the rules of evidence, and all of them, and apparently in all types of cases, because it answers question (3) of the questionnaire:[15] "We have had no experience in this matter." The Commission further states: "It has not been our experience that applying the rules of evidence operates against obtaining an accurate understanding of the facts."

In *New York* the chairman of the Transit Commission [16] carefully answered the questionnaire as follows: "Generally speaking, the policy is to apply the rules of evidence, but this policy is carried out with liberality, in view of the provision of section 20 of the Public Service Law that the Commission 'shall not be bound by the technical rules of evidence.'[17] The ascertainment of the true facts is regarded as more important than the rigid adherence to rules of evidence. Much depends upon the circumstances of the particular case. Frequently, the record is supplemented with the testimony of our own investigators. In making our determinations, emphasis is naturally placed upon the strongest evidence and, in this way, the rules of evidence may be given a certain indirect effect. The insistence, or the reverse, on certain rules of evidence is largely a matter of discretion, depending upon the circumstances of the particular case. The 'hearsay' rule is generally enforced. The 'best evidence' rule is sometimes modified, but is occasionally insisted upon where the party can easily conform to it. Because of varying circumstances, it is impossible to say that any rules are systematically enforced or ignored. In general, the policy is to follow the rules of evidence where this can be done without injustice to lay complainants and without blocking the avenues to the truth.

"The provision of Rule IV, 3, excluding documents unless copies are furnished is frequently waived in the interest of convenience and the ascertainment of the truth.

"I cannot say that, under our practice, I have had any case in my experience where the *omission* to apply the rules of evidence operated against obtaining an accurate understanding of the facts. An absolute disregard of all rules would be undesirable; but these

---

[15] To what extent, if any, have you found in your experience that omission to apply the rules of evidence operates against obtaining an accurate understanding of the facts?

[16] The Metropolitan Division of the Department of Public Service.

[17] See II C *supra*.

rules (designed for juries) may be, in part, relaxed with benefit before an administrative tribunal. The extent of such relaxation depends, of course, upon the character of the rule and upon the special circumstances of the case.

"As our practice is not to apply the rules of evidence without modification, I have in mind no case in my experience where *applying* the rules operated against obtaining an accurate understanding of the facts. In my opinion, however, a rigid application of the rules would have that effect. Lay complainants would often be deprived of the opportunity of showing their substantive rights, if held to rigid rules of evidence, with which they are unfamiliar. Companies or complainants represented by attorneys would not suffer to the same extent, but, even in their case, occasions may arise calling for a relaxation of the rules.

"Undoubtedly the rules of evidence represent the distillation of past experience and wisdom (particularly as applied before juries); and we try to follow them so far as they embody such wisdom and experience as is applicable to our situation. Our aim is to follow them so far as they are sound and to waive them in so far as they seem to become obstacles to ascertaining the true facts. This necessarily involves a considerable exercise of discretion in particular cases."

The Public Service Commission of *New York* states that the rules of evidence are applied "only very generally. The Commission has never ruled that it will apply certain ones and omit certain others." The Commission has ". . . not found that our [its] practice prevents obtaining accurate information. If the rules of evidence were strictly applied, hearings would be extended and justice retarded. In many of our cases, parties in interest are not represented by lawyers, and they can hardly be expected to adhere to rules with which they are not familiar."

In *North Carolina* the Commission frankly states: "Our statute[18] requires that the same rules of evidence shall be enforced in the court of the Corporation Commission as are enforced in the Superior Courts, but our Commission has never adhered strictly to this requirement when the ends of justice demanded a more liberal policy. We apply a great many of the rules, such as the rule against hearsay testimony and the rule as to secondary evidence, but we admit affidavits where the adverse party has an opportunity to answer them and petitions from the people without requirement of proof

---

[18] See II C *supra*.

of signatures. We recall no specific instance where the omission to apply the rules of evidence has operated against obtaining an accurate understanding of the facts. Many petitioners before our Commission come without lawyers and where there are not lawyers on both sides we generally let down the bars, and accept any evidence which we think reliable and that can assist us in arriving at the facts. In such case we are sure that applying the strict rules of evidence would greatly handicap the parties in presenting their case and handicap us in arriving at the facts."

In *Ohio* "there is no strict application of the rules of evidence. Non-application of rules of evidence is made for brevity and a plain statement of facts, which might not otherwise be made." The experience of the Commission is that ". . . omitting a strict application of the rules of evidence does not militate against an accurate understanding of the facts." But the Commission nevertheless states: "Strict application . . . of rules of evidence, no doubt, is a time saver . . ."[19] The Commission comments further: "Generally, since the Commission is a fact-finding body, rather wide latitude is allowed in the offering of testimony. Perhaps the strict application of the rules of evidence obtains in the qualifying of expert witnesses and in the admission of documentary evidence."

The Corporation Commission in *Oklahoma* applies the rules of evidence ". . . so far as practicable. We endeavor to get the facts, as a legislative tribunal, in rate proceedings." The Commission is not bound in such proceedings ". . . by inhibition of rules which would preclude getting at the facts." The Commission chairman amplified the answers further by stating: ". . . In rate matters we assume to sit as a legislative tribunal and cannot be restricted by rules of evidence applicable in the courts. The fundamental conception of this Commission as an agency for developing facts, with the primary purpose of seeing that the public's side of controversies is gotten before this Commission, precludes the strict application of rules of evidence. However, we are not unmindful of the fact that matters tried here may go on appeal to the Supreme Court of the State, or get before Federal tribunals, and hence we do attempt to see that evidence is presented somewhat in accordance with rules applicable to the courts, where that seems to be material. For example, we may receive petitions and

[19] It is not clear why non-application is made for brevity when strict application is a time saver.

CHAP. V] THE RULES OF EVIDENCE 79

letters, but in the absence of the presence of witnesses before the Commission these things can be given little more weight than pleadings in a case. . . . In a tribunal which regards itself as a Commission sitting as we do, under the conception which I have expressed of the office, you would not expect to find the hard and fast rules of evidence as for example existing in criminal proceedings or even in civil proceedings where the court sits primarily as an umpire, or as an agency of the law to apply rules laid down for its guidance. The public utility, or public service commission is, in my opinion, still in an experimental stage and considerable liberality in matters of practice must be permitted, if it is to be of any worthwhile function."

The Public Service Commission of *Pennsylvania* "speaking generally" applies the rules of evidence. "On unimportant points we frequently accept affidavits instead of oral testimony. Hearsay rule is not strictly applied; testimony of one who has interviewed a number of persons as to a business need with which they are directly conversant is frequently accepted instead of requiring those persons to appear and testify. Mere gossip is always excluded." The Commission has "not found that failure to apply rules of evidence in above instances operates against obtaining an accurate understanding of facts by an administrative tribunal, if judgment is used as to how far rules should be relaxed." But the Commission believes "it best to apply rules of evidence, provided they are not enforced so strictly as to require prohibitively expensive methods of establishing of record the necessary and relevant facts."

In *Rhode Island* the "Commission does not adhere to the rules of the submission of evidence before the courts except in a general way. The Commission's intent is to get at all of the facts regardless of whether or not in so doing strict rules of evidence as applied by the courts were used."

In *South Carolina* it is the practice of the Commission to "generally apply all" of the rules of evidence. But the Commission seems to be of the view that applying or not applying the rules of evidence "does not have much effect either way" so far as obtaining an accurate understanding of the facts is concerned.[20] In *Tennessee* "the Commission has not deviated from the ordinary rules of evidence applicable to trials in courts of record in the state

[20] There is no provision in the South Carolina statutes concerning the rules of evidence. II C *supra*.

except by not enforcing the rules of evidence strictly in all cases which come before the Commsision. In other words, no announced policy of a deviation from the rules has been made but the Commission has been somewhat liberal in admitting evidence. It would be impossible to announce in what particulars deviation from the rules has been made."

The Railroad Commission of *Texas* ". . . does not apply the rules of evidence strictly. . . . The only fixed rule . . . is that all evidence is given under oath. Otherwise, the Commission permits examination that would possibly not be accepted in courts. Many things go into our records merely for the benefit that might be derived from the information, rather than adhering strictly to the methods used in court procedure. . . . Practice before the Commission is not restricted to members of the bar."

In *Utah* the chairman of the commission,[21] took pains to prepare the following answers: "(1) As Andy says, 'Yes and no, mostly no.' We pay little attention to the rules of evidence in the course of our investigation of matters submitted. The questions we have to determine are largely social and economic ones, not legal, therefore requiring procedure unknown to the Courts. (2) Yes. We often apply the rules of evidence with respect to wholly immaterial or irrelevant matters. Obviously the admission of such evidence would add nothing to the facts for determination by a regulatory or administrative body. We also rule against evidence that is purely argumentative. (3) Technical rules of evidence under our statute may be disregarded. In practice and procedure their omission, we have found, not only tends to expedite hearings, but affords many witnesses not under the guidance of attorneys greater freedom of expression, which in the main will lead to a better understanding of the facts we ultimately have to determine. Opinion evidence, while generally admitted for the record, oftentimes operates against an accurate understanding of the facts, unless supplemented with the reasons or the facts upon which opinion of the witness is predicated. (4) Strict application of the rules of evidence and the observance of court procedure would in practically all cases defeat the purpose for which public utility commissions were created, that of safe-guarding the public interest and providing for the general welfare. Cases submitted to us are for investigation, rather than for trial. However, that is not saying that in the interest of orderly procedure, and the proper investigation of

[21] Formerly a justice of the supreme court of the state.

CHAP. V] THE RULES OF EVIDENCE 81

a matter submitted, the rules of evidence may not well be sometimes applied."

The Public Service Commission of the State of *Vermont* to the question,"Do you apply the rules of evidence?" answers [22] "Yes." Note that the Vermont statutes permit the Commission to make its own rules of practice.[23]

In *Virginia* the commission applies the rules of evidence ". . . except in rate matters, etc., which are quasi-judicial." But the commission states further: "We are liberal in the application of rules of procedure and admissibility of evidence. We want all the facts, so that a just conclusion may be reached."

In *Washington*, where a rule [24] provides "rules of evidence . . . obtaining in court procedure will be followed in so far as they are appropriate," [25] the Department of Public Works nevertheless states that the rules of evidence are "not generally" applied. "Some testimony is excluded when remote. Rule against hearsay followed to some extent. Vast latitude allowed in opinion testimony. The failure to apply rules of evidence makes the hearing unnecessarily long." The Department does not ". . . think it operates to conceal the actual facts to any extent. The application of strict rules of evidence would make it impossible to ascertain the public sentiment on such questions as the necessity for stage service, etc."

In *West Virginia* the Public Service Commission, referring to the statute [26] freeing it from "the technical rules . . . of evidence" and giving it "such discretion as will facilitate its efforts to understand and learn all the facts bearing upon the right and justice of the matters before it," does "not strictly" apply the rules of evidence. "General rules" are applied ". . . but meticulous adherence with reference to records is not required to expedite investigations." The Commission has not found that omission to apply the rules of evidence operates against obtaining an accurate understanding of the facts. "But the cumbersomeness of regulatory investigations is largely overcome by waiving technical rules of evidence."

In *Wyoming* the commission states that the rules of evidence are applied. "Being a judicial body whose judgments are reviewable

---

[22] In the laconic manner of a distinguished native of that state.
[23] II C *supra*.   [24] III C *supra*.
[25] The Washington statute contains no provision respecting the rules of evidence. II C *supra*.   [26] II C *supra*.

by the Supreme Court, it is necessary. Our statute provides that our hearings be conducted under the provisions of Civil Procedure." In respect of to what extent applying rules operates against obtaining an accurate understanding of the facts, the commission states, "No more so than such procedure so operates in Civil and Equity cases in a Court. We also, of course, apply the rule relative to Judicial Knowledge — of which we necessarily have considerable." [27]

The *Interstate Commerce Commission*, after referring to the judicial decisions holding that the mere admission by an administrative tribunal of matters which under the rules of evidence applicable to judicial proceedings would be deemed incompetent does not invalidate its order, and that the Commission is not bound by the technical rules of procedure or evidence, and that it is not expected nor required that its decisions can be tested by any mathematically correct rules, adds that the courts have held that the Commission ". . . must observe some of the fundamental rules such as giving to the parties the opportunity of cross-examination . . .", and adds further: "It, of course, may be generally stated that we do not apply the rules of evidence strictly . . ."; and the Commission cannot say ". . . that we have ever found that by so doing we have been unable to arrive at a correct understanding of the facts." [28]

The *Federal Trade Commission*, "in practice . . . has intended to receive only legally competent evidence and to base its findings as to the facts only upon such evidence." [29]

Thus of the thirty-eight commissions from which replies were received, but four, those in New Mexico, Vermont, Wyoming,

[27] The Wyoming reply seems inconsistent with the statute, II C *supra*, providing, "all hearings and investigations before the commission shall be conducted under such rules as the commission may prescribe and adopt." There is an additional statutory provision, however, §§ 94–162, dealing with appeals to the court from orders of the commission. It reads: "The provisions of the code of civil procedure of this state shall, so far as applicable and not in conflict with the provisions of this chapter, apply to all appellate proceedings, held or had under the provisions hereof."

[28] In 1908, in its report to Congress, the Commission said: "It is, perhaps, not too much to say that not a single case arising before the Commission could be properly decided if the complainant, the railroad, or the Commission were bound by the rules of evidence applying to the introduction of testimony in courts." Twenty-second Annual Report of the I. C. C. (1908), p. 10.

[29] But, as stated *supra*, the Circuit Court of Appeals for the Second Circuit (See John Bene & Sons, Inc. *v.* Federal Trade Commission, IV B *supra*)

CHAP. V] THE RULES OF EVIDENCE 83

and the Federal Trade Commission, report a fixed practice of applying the rules of evidence. Of the others, the Oklahoma commission applies them so far as practicable, though not in rate proceedings, the Illinois commission so far as practicable, and the Arizona, Hawaii, Maine, South Carolina, and Virginia commissions generally apply the rules, though Virginia, again, does not in rate matters. As to the rest of the commissions reporting, while there are variations in the practice from state to state, and while some of the commissions are freer than others, and it is therefore not possible with entire accuracy to set forth in a phrase a rule characterizing all, it is perhaps fair to say that none of them applies the rules of evidence with the full vigor and strictness of courts, and that all indulge in a substantial freedom and seek the facts upon which their orders are founded much according to discretion rather than rule. When comment is made upon the topic, there seems to be agreement, except in Hawaii, that in rate cases and in investigations by the commissions themselves, proceedings of a legislative character, the rules of evidence are of little or no value. But even among the commissions thus, in general, not applying the rules, exceptions are to be noted, Colorado at times applying the hearsay rule, Connecticut insisting upon relevancy, the District of Columbia limiting the cross-examination to the scope of the direct, Iowa generally observing "essential rules," Nebraska applying the hearsay rule, and applying the rules to "direct evidence and exhibits" and in hearings between railroads represented by attorneys, New Jersey applying the rules in public hearings, the New York Transit Commission generally enforcing the hearsay rule, North Carolina the hearsay and best evidence rules, Pennsylvania excluding mere gossip, Texas requiring an oath, Utah excluding irrelevant and argumentative matter, and the Interstate Commerce Commission allowing the parties the right of cross-examination. In Georgia and North Carolina the departure from the rules is in the face of a contravening statute, and in Washington, where the statute requires following the rules obtaining in court procedure so far as "appropriate," the Commission apparently finds them inappropriate.

permits the Commission to "receive and consider evidence even though legally incompetent if of a kind that usually affects fair-minded men in the conduct of their daily and more important affairs."

Contrast also the statement of Henderson, *Federal Trade Commission* (1924), p. 64, quoted in I *supra*.

To the extent that there was comment in the answers to the questionnaire upon what particular rules especially are not applied, it appears that those discountenanced are the hearsay rule, Arizona, District of Columbia, Georgia, Hawaii, Missouri, North Carolina, and Pennsylvania; the best evidence rule, Arizona, Missouri, New York Transit Commission; the opinion rule, Hawaii and Washington; and the rule requiring a showing of the relation of offered exhibits to the issues, North Carolina (admission of people's petitions without proof of signatures).

CHAPTER VI

SUMMARIES AND COMPARISONS

A. *Legislation.* A comparison of the statutes in effect governing the activities of the commissions in the fields in which a study of the statutes as such was made [1] indicates seven types of legislation: (1) The federal statutes relating to the Interstate Commerce Commission,[2] and the state statutes [3] authorizing the conduct of hearings in such manner as will best conduce to the dispatch of business and the ends of justice. (2) The federal statutes governing the activities of the Public Service Commission of the District of Columbia,[4] and the state statutes [5] giving the commissions power to adopt reasonable and proper rules to regulate the mode and manner of their hearings. (3) The federal statutes concerning the Federal Trade Commission [6] and the Bureau of Immigration,[7] and the state statutes [8] which provide for tribunals but which are silent concerning the manner of conducting hearings, that is, contain no provisions which either expressly or by implication relate to the application of the rules of evidence. (4) State statutes [9] which in addition to authorizing the commissions to adopt reasonable rules to regulate the manner of their hearings, provide that substantial compliance with the statutes shall be sufficient, and that orders shall not be declared void for any omission of a technical nature. (5) State statutes [10] which, in addition to authorizing the commis-

---

[1] The tax statutes were considered only so far as reference was made thereto in the judicial decisions. [2] II A *supra.*

[3] Of Iowa, Minnesota, Kentucky and Oklahoma, II C 4 *supra.*

[4] II C 1 *supra.*

[5] Of Kansas, Michigan, Montana, Nebraska, Ohio, Oregon, Pennsylvania, Tennessee, Texas, Wyoming, South Dakota, Nevada, and New Mexico, II C 1 *supra.*

[6] II B *supra.* [7] II D *supra.*

[8] Of Connecticut, Indiana, Louisiana, Massachusetts, Mississippi, South Carolina, and Washington, II C 7 *supra.*

[9] Of Alabama and Wisconsin, II C 2 *supra.*

[10] Of Arizona, Arkansas, California, Colorado, Hawaii, Idaho, Illinois, Maryland, Missouri, New Hampshire, New Jersey, New York, North Dakota, Rhode Island, Utah, and West Virginia, II C 3 *supra.*

sions to prescribe rules of practice, expressly relieve them of the "technical rules of evidence" and of formalities, or also permit them to exercise "discretion" with a view to "doing justice." (6) State statutes requiring the commissions to apply the rules of evidence.[11] (7) A state statute [12] requiring the commission to observe the common and statute-law rules of evidence as observed by courts when called upon to render judgment in its capacity as a court of record.

B. *Rules.* The rules relating to manner of taking evidence fall into five classes: (1) Those making no provision except that it is apparently intended that evidence taken shall be relevant and material.[13] (2) Rules [14] providing that the commission shall not be bound by the "technical rules of evidence." (3) Rules [15] providing for disregard of errors which shall not affect the substantial rights of the parties. (4) Rules [16] permitting the commission to take [17] such evidence as it may think pertinent, admissible and material, or [18] appropriate. (5) Rules [19] providing expressly that the rules of evidence shall be the same as in civil actions in court.[20]

C. *Judicial Decisions.* The courts state that the rules of evidence are not to be applied in the hearings of administrative tribunals because: [21] (1) The investigatory, legislative, supervisory, and regulatory aspects of the work of the tribunals are such that the application of rules of evidence would hamper, if not frustrate or render fruitless, such functions.[22] (2) The commissions are administrative in nature.[23] (3) A reparation order has only the effect

[11] Florida, Georgia, Maine, and North Carolina, II C 5 *supra*.
[12] Of Virginia, II C 6 *supra*.
[13] Rules of the Interstate Commerce Commission, III A *supra*, of the Federal Trade Commission, III B *supra*, and of the United States Bureau of Immigration, III D *supra*.
[14] Of the Illinois Commission, III C *supra*.
[15] Of the Commission in New Mexico, III C *supra*.
[16] In Iowa, and Washington, III C *supra*.
[17] In Iowa.   [18] In Washington.
[19] Of the Public Utilities Commission of Maine, III C *supra*.
[20] The Supreme Judicial Court of Maine.
[21] Some of the courts give more than one reason.
[22] Interstate Commerce Commission *v.* Baird, IV A *supra*; Steenerson *v.* Great Northern Ry. Co., and Steamboat Canal Co. *v.* Garson, public service commission cases, IV C *supra*; and People *v.* Hicks, a tax case, IV D *supra*.
[23] Interstate Commerce Commission *v.* Louisville & N. R. Co., IV A *supra*; Chicago & Northwestern R. Co. *v.* Railroad Commission, IV C *supra*; and People *ex rel.* Schabacker *v.* State Assessors, a tax case, IV D *supra*.

CHAP. VI] THE RULES OF EVIDENCE 87

of prima facie evidence.[24] (4) The rules of evidence are objectionable as mechanical and mathematical.[25] (5) It is necessary to dispense with the rules of evidence.[26] (6) Evidence of the kind that usually affects fair-minded men in the conduct of their daily and more important affairs is sufficient for administrative tribunals.[27] (7) The expertness of administrative officials makes unnecessary the application of the rules of evidence.[28] (8) The fact of *de novo* hearings on appeal warrants relaxing the rules in the tribunal hearings.[29] (9) Such is the intent of legislatures.[30] (10) It saves time.[31] (11) It saves expense.[32] (12) Hearings are "fair," notwithstanding non-application of the rules; it is not bad faith or improper conduct to violate them.[33] (13) It is not denial of due process not to conduct the hearings under the rules of evidence.[34] (14) The summary nature of the proceedings warrants dispensing with the rules of evidence.[35]

D. *The Practice in the Commissions.* The commissions' hearings should be conducted without strict application of the rules of

[24] Spiller *v.* Atchison, Topeka & Santa Fe Ry., an Interstate Commerce Commission case, IV A *supra.*

[25] Western Paper Makers' Chemical Company *v.* United States, Beaumont S. L. & W. R. Co. *v.* United States, and Montrose Oil Refining Company *v.* St. Louis-San Francisco R. Co., Interstate Commerce Commission cases, IV A *supra.*

[26] Beaumont S. L. & W. R. Co. *v.* United States, an Interstate Commerce Commission case, IV A *supra;* and Western Union Tel. Co. *v.* Dodge County, and People *v.* Hicks, tax cases, IV D *supra.*

[27] John Bene & Son *v.* Federal Trade Commission, IV B *supra.*

[28] Chicago & Northwestern R. Co. *v.* Railroad Commission, IV C *supra;* United States *v.* Uhl, and Chin Shee *v.* White, the last two alien cases, IV E 9 (a) *supra.*

[29] Duluth St. R. Co. *v.* Railroad Commission, St. Louis Southwestern Ry. Co. *v.* Stewart, a public service commission case, and Atchison, T. & S. F. R. *v.* Public Service Commission of Kansas, all IV C *supra.*

[30] Lindsey *v.* Pub. Util. Comm., Schuykill Ry. Co. *v.* Pub. Serv. Comm., both IV C *supra*, and People *ex rel.* Schabacker *v.* State Assessors, a tax case, IV D *supra.*

[31] People *ex rel.* Schabacker *v.* State Assessors, IV D *supra*, and United States *v.* Uhl, an alien case, IV E 9 (a) *supra.*

[32] People *ex rel.* Schabacker *v.* State Assessors, and People *ex rel.* Hunt *v.* Priest, both tax cases, IV D *supra.*

[33] Cahan *v.* Carr, Chin Shee *v.* White, and Tang Tun *v.* Edsell, alien cases, IV E *supra.*

[34] Moy Yoke Shue *v.* Johnson, an alien case, IV E *supra.*

[35] People *ex rel.* Schabacker *v.* State Assessors, IV D *supra*, and United States *ex rel.* Ng Wing *v.* Brough, an alien case, IV E *supra.*

evidence, according to the replies to the questionnaire, because: [36] (1) A fuller and more accurate understanding of the facts is thus obtained.[37] (2) The hearings are expedited.[38] (3) It is less expensive.[39] (4) The rules of evidence are "useless technical requirements in our judicial procedure,"[40] and the ". . . intent is to get at all of the facts regardless of whether or not in so doing the strict rules of evidence as applied by the courts . . ." are used [41] and "the ascertainment of the true facts is regarded as more important than the rigid adherence to rules of evidence."[42] (5) It is necessary, in order to get public sentiment on such questions as necessity for service.[43] (6) Cases are frequently presented by parties acting without counsel.[44] (7) The commissioners are more expert than juries in weighing evidence.[45] (8) The commission "represents the public generally,"[46] and "the primary purpose of seeing that the public's side of controversies . . ." is placed before the commission [47] will be thus better effected and ". . . the purpose for which public utilities commissions were created, that of safeguarding the public interest and providing for the general welfare . . ."[48] better carried out. (9) ". . . The findings of a Commission, not being forever final and binding upon the parties, need not be (so) hedged by inflexible rules."[49] (10) The rules of evidence were designed for juries rather than commissions.[50] (11) The commission sits ". . . as a legislative tribunal . . ."[51] and ". . . exercises legislative powers and is a branch of the legislative power of the state. . . ."[52] (12) The determination of questions ". . .

[36] The reasons given by the various commissions for not applying the rules of evidence are, of course, somewhat differently expressed. An attempt is here made, for the purpose of comparison, to give in a few words a fair description of reasons in substance the same. Some commissions give more than one reason. Some give none. See V *supra* for resumé of the answers of each commission to the questionnaire.

[37] Arkansas, Colorado, Connecticut, District of Columbia, Illinois, Maryland, Minnesota, New Jersey, North Carolina, Ohio, Oklahoma, and Utah.

[38] Connecticut, Georgia, Massachusetts, Nevada, New York (Public Service Commission), Ohio, and Utah.

[39] District of Columbia, and Pennsylvania.

[40] Georgia.

[41] Rhode Island.

[42] New York (Transit Commission).

[43] Washington.

[44] Hawaii, Maine, Missouri, New York (both Public Service Commission and Transit Commission), North Carolina, Texas, and Utah.

[45] Missouri. [46] Missouri. [47] Oklahoma. [48] Utah. [49] Missouri.
[50] New York (Transit Commission). [51] Oklahoma. [52] Missouri.

CHAP. VI] THE RULES OF EVIDENCE 89

largely social and economic . . . not legal . . ." requires ". . . procedure unknown to the courts." [53] (13) The rules of evidence "work disadvantageously" and "better results" are obtained without the rules, and "if strict rules of evidence were applied, such as are in force in the Courts, the record of hearings would be limited and not serve the general purpose for which the Board was created." [54]

E. *Comparison of the Courts' and Commissions' Reasons for not Applying the Rules of Evidence.* There are some identities between the reasons given by the courts in sanctioning non-application of the rules of evidence and the reasons given by the commissions. Thus the judicial comments that the investigatory, legislative, supervisory and regulatory aspects of the work of the commissions require freedom from the rules of evidence, parallel in substance the commissions' comments that they represent the public generally and have to determine questions largely social and economic by procedure unknown to the courts. The views of the courts that the rules of evidence would hamper if not frustrate the functions of the tribunals, and that the rules are objectionable as mechanical or mathematical, are not unlike those of the commissions that a fuller and more accurate understanding of the facts is obtained without application of the rules. The expertness of administrative officials as compared with juries is commented upon both by the courts and the commissions. Both emphasize that the omission to apply the rules of evidence expedites the hearings.

On the whole, while the courts themselves are at times bluntly opposed to the use of the rules of evidence, as indicated in the statements that they would hamper, if not frustrate, administrative tribunal activities, or make them fruitless, they are perhaps somewhat less sharply adverse than the commissions, as evidenced in the comments in Georgia, Rhode Island, and New York, describing the rules of evidence as useless technical requirements, and indicating that ascertainment of the facts is more important than adherence to the rules. Such language seems to indicate that the commissions regard compliance with the rules of evidence as an empty ceremony unrelated to fact finding, but which the courts nevertheless feel obliged to perform.

F. *Comparison of the Judicial Decisions in each Class of Cases, in respect of the Rules of Evidence Infringed by the Commissions and*

[53] Utah.
[54] Indiana, Maine, and New Jersey.

Types of Matter Admitted. The surveys and summaries [55] of judicial decisions set forth above indicate that the Interstate Commerce Commission, with judicial sanction, contents itself largely with infringement of the hearsay rule, the Federal Trade Commission [56] with violation of the hearsay rule, the best evidence rule, and the opinion rule. The state public service commissions have judicial support in disregarding the hearsay rule, the best evidence rule, and the opinion rule, the tax commissions in respect of violation of the hearsay and opinion rules, and the rule against former judicial determinations. The immigration tribunals are permitted to go further, to violate in addition to those above mentioned, the rules concerning impeachment, other crimes, and the testimony of wife against husband.

As to types of matter admitted, the Interstate Commerce Commission cases sanction unidentified signatures, hearsay data supporting claims for reparation, and hearsay in the form of evidence taken in another cause. The Federal Trade Commission receives,[57] with judicial approval, lay opinions as to the uses of solutions, hearsay as to events and correspondence not within a witness' knowledge, secondary evidence as to the contents of books, and testimony immaterial because not connected. The state public service commissions are allowed to receive carriers' reports, engineers' reports, testimony and data in other causes, letters, and copies of contracts. The tax cases sanction the use of carriers' reports, commercial ratings, investors' manuals, statements in deeds, and affidavits. The alien cases warrant the reception of common knowledge, press reports, letters, interviews and newspaper clippings, affidavits of prostitutes, and the statements of their "customers."

The decisions in reference to the activities of the Interstate Commerce Commission are, of the classes of cases considered, the most conservative. It is there that the use of the commission's own information not formally proved at the hearing, or the use of anything as evidence which is not introduced as such, is strictly forbidden by the United States Supreme Court; that is to say, it is there that that Court insists that the parties shall have a hearing in the real and legal sense of that word. The state courts are less conservative, warranting in one instance, in a tax case, the use of

[55] At the end of the discussion of each class of cases in IV *supra*.
[56] It is to be remembered that there was but one case.
[57] In the one case.

evidence taken secretly from presumably prejudiced witnesses, and in others, in the state public service commission cases, seemingly going so far as to dispense with the introduction of evidence, or as to dispense with introduction, provided the parties are advised of the matter considered by the commission, or where the parties know of the matter and have opportunity to test, explain or refute it. The federal courts in the alien cases are equally liberal, including within their rulings the denial of the right of cross-examination.[58] It seems fair to state that in warranting the reception of "any evidence worthy of credit" and evidence for what it is "worth," and the conduct of hearings free from "any of the common-law rules," the courts in the alien cases go substantially further in sanctioning infringement of the rules of evidence than do the courts in the other classes of cases.

[58] There is apparently no decision in the United States Supreme Court going this far, and United States *ex rel.* Bilokumsky *v.* Tod, IV E 1 *supra*, indicates that the Supreme Court would not go so far.

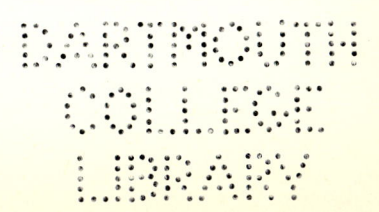

CHAPTER VII

CONCLUSIONS

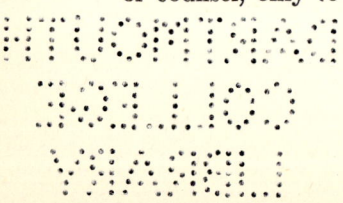

It was suggested at the outset of this study that it was aimed to discover what rules of evidence are not applied, why they are not applied, and, so far as possible, with what effect. So far as the views of legislatures, commissions as rule makers, commissions in practice, and courts reviewing the hearings of commissioners are concerned, these questions have, in effect, been answered in the summaries and comparisons above set forth. It is sufficient here to state, by way of brief conclusion, that, with a few exceptions, legislatures and commissions lean far toward, if they do not embrace in full, the so-called popular view, referred to in the Introduction, to the effect that "the jury trial rules have had their day" even in the courts, and that to transplant them to new fields would be "an error amounting to a folly." The courts themselves, reviewing the refusal of commissions to apply the rules of evidence, have, with exceptions, sustained the commissions. The rules which the commissions refuse to apply, as will have been seen from the resumés and comparisons above, are the hearsay rule, the best evidence rule, the opinion rule, the rules with reference to impeachment, the rule forbidding testimony of spouse against spouse, the rule against the admission of one act or crime to prove another, the rules confining testimony to that which has been demonstrated, by connection with the subject matter of the case, to be material, and the rule forbidding the admission of judgments in one proceeding as evidence of facts in issue in another. There is no explicit definition, either by legislatures, rule makers, commissions in comments upon their practice, or courts, of "the technical rules" of evidence, or other like phrases so frequently used to discountenance the rules of evidence as applied by courts. But it may fairly be concluded, in view of the frequent use of such terms in connection with commission refusals, and judicial sanction thereof, to apply the rules above enumerated, that those rules are the rules which the courts and commissions have in mind as "the technical rules of evidence." Of such rules the ones most commonly invoked by parties or counsel, only to meet rejection by commissions and reviewing courts, are the hearsay rule, the best evidence rule, and the opinion rule.

Why legislatures, commissions, and courts have taken this stand against application of the rules of evidence has also been made sufficiently apparent in the comments above to make it unnecessary to do more here than briefly to restate that it is thought that the problems to be solved by administrative tribunals are so different from those commonly confronting courts that methods unknown to the courts must be followed, and that application of the rules of evidence would gravely limit, if not frustrate, the commissions' work, and that the result of freeing the commissions from the rules of evidence is wholesomely to enhance the efficiency of their work. In particular, as to the effect, it is believed that the conduct of the activities, including the hearings, of the commissions, without the rules of evidence, saves money, time, and trouble, and leads to a better understanding of the facts. It is the view, moreover, of both courts and commissioners, certainly of commissioners, that the latter are experts who may, on that account, be trusted to seek facts for the foundation of their orders without the aid of the rules which courts have believed necessary to assure an honest, accurate, and unprejudiced assembling of information for juries, indeed for judges. Commissioners, it is believed, can weigh the evidence, whatever its nature and however informally presented, better than courts. Their expertness enables them to know the worth of hearsay, the probable authenticity of unidentified signatures, the comparative value of evidence taken in other causes — without being confused or misled by, or obliged to sift out, the collateral issues involved; to know the value of the conclusions of lay witnesses without presentation of the data upon which they are based; to understand how far to give credence to matters not within a witness' knowledge; to judge of the correctness of secondary evidence as to the contents of books; to know whether or not to consider testimony not shown to be connected with the case; to judge the value of letters and telegrams and copies of contracts; to sense the accuracy of commercial ratings, investors' manuals, recitals in deeds, interviews, newspaper clippings; to know the worth of common knowledge; to understand the statistical reports of carriers, and the scientific reports of engineers without examination of the makers; to give proper weight to the affidavits of prostitutes and the *ex parte* statements of their "customers"; to evaluate impeachment without explanation; to tell how far to treat contradictions as affirmative evidence; to value the testimony of wife against husband; to know to what extent proof of the commission of one act is proof of the commission of a similar one; to take evidence for what it is worth without discrimination at the outset as to competency; and to act dependably and fairly upon their own information undisclosed to parties or to reviewing courts — all better than judges and juries. Commissioners have prescience indeed. This is not an indictment of commissioners; it is a recital of their own doings with the rules of evidence, told by themselves, and sanctioned by reviewing courts.

How sound are these views concerning commissions, and how far warranted is their practice of not applying the rules of evidence? It is the experience of trial judges that when counsel fail to insist upon the rules of evidence, hearings are prolonged, not expedited, and that the record becomes so bulky and diffuse and confused in its mixture of the material and the immaterial, of the dependable and the undependable, that an apt and sound decision of the cause is made more difficult, not easier, for either juries, or judges sitting alone. For courts, the rules of evidence have been not a fetish nor an empty ceremony but, tested by experience, a handy scalpel to dissect within the field of operation defined by the pleadings, and an aseptic against influences disturbing to the mind. To courts, desirous of deciding causes upon evidence of whose relation to the issues the trier of fact is consciously aware, it is desirable to pass upon the admissibility of evidence at the time it is presented in order that the mind may act definitely and with finality upon it, and exclude from consideration, so far as possible, what is immaterial, confusing, or likely to disturb. Sharp rulings, definitely made at the time of presentation of evidence, aid the trial court, counsel, and reviewing tribunal toward a meeting of minds upon what actuates a decision. The *pro forma* reception of evidence promotes decisions on "hunch." [1]

[1] It is of interest to note that business men, without being conscious that they are doing so, often apply the rules of evidence in ordinary transactions, in particular the hearsay and the best evidence rules and, frequently, the rules against conclusions. A banker considering a loan will not be content with the statement of the applicant that John Doe has estimated the value of the applicant's property at so many dollars. He will wish to talk with John Doe and question him about the basis of his valuation; if the applicant, by way of offering security, states that he has a contract or that he owns a mortgage, the banker will not be content either with this secondary evidence of the contents of such documents or with the applicant's conclusion as to their legal meaning. He will wish to see the originals.

If the rules of evidence are common-sense ways of determining whether to consider offered proof, why should they not be of value to one tribunal as well as to another? Is it possible that commissioners have fallen into the error of calling a rule technical if it takes pains to apply it? Is it possible that instead of desiring the facts regardless of the rules, they avoid the rules regardless of the facts, that they overvalue speed and the saving of expense? Are we indeed faced, in the complexity of present-day life, with the necessity of regarding speedy decisions as sounder than sound slow ones?

Discriminations, of course, must be made. Frequently, the best evidence rule can be dispensed with without serious threat to the dependability of evidence. Modern mechanical methods and regularity in accounting and office practice are in many cases a "circumstantial guaranty of the verity" of copies of letters and other documents sufficient to warrant their use both by courts and administrative tribunals. The disfavor of the law towards the testimony of spouse against spouse is predicated much more upon the objection to disturbing family confidence than upon distrust of the evidence as such. The certified record of conviction of keeping a disorderly house is probably dependable evidence of being connected with a house of prostitution and sharing the benefit from the earnings of a prostitute. Evidence not connected by formal proof, or signatures and letters not formally authenticated, may be dependably warranted by circumstances. Experienced administrative officials should be able to determine when not to give credence to gossip or rumor, or to conclusions and opinions uttered without expert qualification. Many cases also have sufficient competent evidence to sustain orders, and experience, without doubt, does aid administrative officials in avoiding the influence of incompetent matter.

The sacrifice of cross-examination, however, seems serious. It is not impossible to *reject* hearsay after having heard it, that is, to determine to give it *no* weight. But if it is to be *relied on*, how far is the trier of fact to give it worth? He hears X testify that Y said Z happened. How *can* the trier of fact, whatever his expertness, be he juror, judge, or commissioner, know whether Z did happen, unless he knows something of Y's opportunity to know, capacity to observe, and ability correctly to remember and to tell of the happening of Z. How *can* a commissioner know the value of an engineer's report [2] without examining the engineer, indeed

[2] Duluth St. R. Co. *v.* Railroad Commission, IV C *supra*.

without hearing him examined by a party or counsel more anxious even than the commissioner to know the reliability of the report? The value of adversary methods is not merely to the parties. The heat of the contest melts out the dross for the tribunal. How *can* the commissioner know the worth of the statement of an alleged prostitute's "customer"[3] without seeing and hearing the customer? If the customer was in error as to identity of the alien an erroneous deportation will follow; and ". . . deportation becomes as to aliens who have established a domicile here a decree of perpetual banishment and exile — regardless of fixed family and business ties and connections; and it more clearly carries a heavy burden of 'possible human woe.'"[4] It is not wholly the warrant of an oath that makes the presence of a witness before a tribunal important; it is much more the opportunity for judging from demeanor and by cross-examination the opportunity of the witness to know what is claimed to be known, and his capacity for observation, memory, and statement.

The right of cross-examination is denied wherever hearsay is admitted, and this is often, as has been pointed out above. It happens not only in the alien cases,[5] but also in tax cases,[6] and in public service commission hearings.[7] Cross-examination is at times denied by the commissions with the sanction of the courts where the commissions have had the benefit of direct examination; the parties are thus forbidden to test the validity of the direct examination, for their own benefit and that of the tribunal.[8]

[3] United States *ex rel.* Ng Wing *v.* Brough, IV E 9 (a) *supra.*
[4] Denison, J., in Browne *v.* Zurbrick, 45 F. (2d) 931, 932 (c.c.a. 6th, 1930).
[5] White *v.* Chan Wy Sheung, where the written statement of a father not produced as a witness, this being material evidence against the claim of an alien that he was the foreign-born son of a native-born Chinese, was admitted, and the alien excluded; United States *ex rel.* Smith *v.* Curran where a widow and her minor son were excluded upon what might be termed double hearsay, telegrams containing the alleged statements of third parties; numerous other alien cases collected in IV E *supra.*
[6] Pratt *v.* Raymond, IV D *supra*, where a board of assessors acted upon evidence obtained by its members in secrecy from complainant's business rivals.
[7] Steamboat Canal Co. *v.* Garson, a water rate case, where testimony and data in another case were received; Chicago & Northwestern R. Co. *v.* Railroad Commission, a rate and reparation case, where carriers' reports were received; Duluth Street R. Co. *v.* Railroad Commission, a rate case, where engineers' reports were admitted; all IV C *supra.*
[8] This was the case in Chin Ah Yoke *v.* White, IV E *supra*, where deportation of an alien as a prostitute was made upon the testimony of a witness who

CHAP. VII] THE RULES OF EVIDENCE 97

If the reception of hearsay testimony and the denial of the right of cross-examination threaten fairness of hearing and dependability of decision, much more so does actual denial of hearing under the guise of relaxation of the rules of evidence or of the formalities of judicial procedure. This has been discountenanced by the United States Supreme Court,[9] where, speaking through Mr. Justice Lamar, the Court, though recognizing that the Interstate Commerce Commission is not limited to the strict rules of evidence, nevertheless held it to the imperative ". . . obligation to preserve the essential rules of evidence by which rights are asserted or defended . . .," and forbade the commissioners "to act upon their own information as could jurors in primitive days," and where, speaking through Mr. Justice Brandeis, the Court stated [10] that ". . . a finding without evidence is beyond the power of the Commission. Papers in the Commission's files are not always evidence in the case. . . . Nothing can be treated as evidence which is not introduced as such." The same Court ruled similarly in an alien case,[11] where, as pointed out, failure by an immigration inspector to place in the record an item of evidence favorable to the alien was held to render the hearing unfair. Such denial of hearing has also been forbidden by the United States Circuit Court of Appeals for the Ninth Circuit,[12] and by the Supreme Court of Kansas,[13] where in the case reviewed *supra*, involving a certificate of con-

was not held for cross-examination. In United States *ex rel.* Ng Wing *v.* Brough, IV E *supra*, where the statements of "customers" that they had had immoral relations for pay with an alien ordered deported for practicing prostitution subsequent to entry were sanctioned, the same being testified to by an inspector, the Circuit Court of Appeals of the United States for the Second Circuit expressly recognized that "Receiving statements of the character here received necessarily denies the opportunity of cross-examination; but the law permits, in a summary proceeding such as this, that such statements be received for what they are worth, with knowledge of the fact that there was no cross-examination. . . ." It is fair to state that in this case, according to the court, there was evidence, apart from the *ex parte* testimony, to support the findings.

[9] Interstate Commerce Commission *v.* Louisville & N. R. Co., IV A *supra*.
[10] United States *v.* Abilene & S. R. Co., IV A *supra*. As a result of this case, it will be remembered, Rule XIII of the Commission, under which matter in carriers' reports on file was being used without introduction in evidence, was altered.
[11] Kwock Jan Fat *v.* White, IV E 6 *supra*.
[12] Whitfield *v.* Hanges, IV E 6 *supra*.
[13] Atchison, T. & S. F. R. Co. *v.* Public Service Commission of Kansas, IV C *supra*.

venience and necessity, though it was held that the commission may gather its facts informally and avail itself of reports and data gathered by its own staff, nevertheless it was also held that ". . . it is only fair that all such facts, data, and reports, wheresoever gleaned, should be presented in public, so that the parties to be affected may show, if they can, by cross-examination or otherwise, that such data and reports are either inaccurate, falacious, or incomplete or not of controlling significance." [14]

These views seem sound. It is of course at times difficult to draw a line between either the taking of a view by commissioners for the purpose of better understanding evidence, or the expert information and capacity of commissioners which also enables them the better to understand and decide, on the one hand, and on the other the actual gathering of information by commissioners and decision of causes thereon without submitting such information to the record and the parties. But if by a hearing is meant, as outside the field of Oriental justice it is thought to mean, the right to know, and to be heard concerning, the evidence relied on, and the right to argue to the very mind which is to act upon such evidence, such a line must be drawn, and, it is submitted, can be drawn, by commissions, as it has been drawn by courts. Certainly no practical difficulty stands in the way of drawing the line against action by commissions upon papers in their files, carriers' and engineers' reports, and other such data, without submitting the same to the record and to the scrutiny of the parties and of the reviewing tribunal. Not only is a fair hearing not had, in the absence of such procedure, but a fair review cannot be made. Unless evidence acted upon is introduced, the reviewing tribunal cannot know of it.

But the rulings and practice are otherwise in numerous instances. Thus, as has been shown above,[15] the supreme court of Wisconsin supported an order of the Railroad Commission in a rate and reparation case where it was asserted, as against the order of the Commission, that it was made in part upon evidence [16] not produced at the hearing and not brought to the attention of the appellant railroad company, and that hence due process was denied; and the court held that it was not necessary that these "public

---

[14] See also, to the same effect, Wichita R. & Light Co. *v.* Court of Industrial Relations, IV C *supra*.

[15] Chicago & Northwestern R. Co. *v.* Railroad Commission, IV C *supra*.

[16] Reports and tariffs of other railroads made to the State Board of Assessors and to the Railroad Commission.

CHAP. VII] THE RULES OF EVIDENCE 99

documents" be formally offered in evidence before the Commission, or certified up on review, that all parties know of the existence of such documents and, in respect to the contention that the findings and order of the Commission rested upon evidence taken in the absence of and without notice to the appellant, ". . . Doubtless the Commission is not required to proceed in this as in other respects with the strict formalities which obtain in courts. . . ."[17] The same court in a rate case [18] held, upon the faith of the previous decision, that it was proper for the Commission to consider a cost appraisal, made by engineers of the Commission, though it was not formally offered in evidence, and notwithstanding the fact that the engineers making it were not sworn as witnesses at the hearing, although the court did recognize that ". . . of course common fairness would dictate that the plaintiff be advised of the appraisal . . . if the Commission intended to use such figures as a basis for decision"; also, as pointed out above, the supreme court of Minnesota in a rate case,[19] in defining the scope of judicial review, said that the Railroad and Warehouse Commission need not base its decision, as does a trial court, wholly upon evidence which can be submitted for review. There was further noted above a similar ruling in a tax case,[20] where the supreme court of Illinois sustained an assessment made upon evidence obtained by the assessors in secrecy, and in an alien case,[21] where the Circuit Court of Appeals for the Ninth Circuit sustained the introduction into the record, certified to the reviewing court in habeas corpus proceedings, of data apparently submitted also to the Secretary of Labor but not a part of the record made at the hearing before the immigration inspector.

It is submitted that these cases sanction what is in effect not mere relaxation of the rules of evidence or of the formalities of court procedure, but denial of hearing.

It is to be conceded that some discrimination must be made

---

[17] Note that though the appellant railroad company in this case may have known of the existence of such documents in the files of the State Board of Assessors and the Railroad Commission, it does not appear that it knew or could have known which of such documents were the ones which moved the Commission to make its order; and the reviewing tribunal must have been equally in the dark.
[18] Duluth Street R. Co. v. Railroad Commission, IV C supra.
[19] Steenerson v. Great Northern Ry. Co., IV C supra.
[20] Pratt v. Raymond, IV D supra.
[21] Chin Shee v. White, IV E 9 (c) supra.

between the different kinds of work of the commissions. In determining whether or not to issue a certificate of convenience and necessity for the construction or extension of railroads, or the operation of motor-bus lines, the problem is not unlike that which might confront a legislature in acting upon a bill for a special charter for a railroad. Legislatures not only must, but undoubtedly should, act upon public opinion as well as upon facts. Indeed, public opinion is for legislatures a controlling fact. And whether convenience requires, or necessity demands, a new or extended railroad, must and should be ascertained by a public service commission in part upon public opinion in the locality to be served. This probably warrants the receipt by such commissions of opinions and conclusions in letters from business men, commercial clubs and other like organizations, commenting upon the present service or the need of new or added facilities.[22] The so-called supervisory duties of the commissions with reference, for example, to adequacy of facilities, probably also present problems best solved by informal investigations and hearings.[23] Rate cases, emphasized in the replies of the commissioners to the questionnaire herein, also present questions to an extent legislative in character. But it is submitted that even in such cases there should not be denial of hearing by action upon actual data not introduced into the record.

Much emphasis is placed, in support of the popular view as to the rules of evidence, upon the proposition that the causes considered by administrative tribunals are not adversary in nature. This also requires discrimination. Hearings for the fixing of rates, or upon application for certificates of convenience and necessity, are not adversary in the sense that a trial between parties in court over property or liberty ordinarily is, although it is to be noted that the effect of rate orders upon the property rights of corporations, and thereby of stockholders, is direct and important, and fairness and accuracy of hearing and decision should be a desired end, if not a wholly attainable one. But reparation cases are adversary in character, as also are proceedings for the division of joint rates. The United States Supreme Court, speaking through Mr. Justice Brandeis, has so stated: ". . . Every proceeding is adversary, in substance, if it may result in an order in favor of one carrier as

[22] Such was the situation in Atchison, T. &. S. F. R. Co. *v.* Public Service Commission of Kansas, IV C *supra*.

[23] Such was the case of St. Louis Southwestern Ry. Co. *v.* Stewart, IV C *supra*, with reference to the construction of a new passenger station.

CHAP. VII] THE RULES OF EVIDENCE 101

against another. Nor was the proceeding under review any the less an adversary one, because the primary purpose of the Commission was to protect the public interest through making possible the continued operation of the Orient system."[24] Of the Interstate Commerce and public service commission cases reviewed above several were adversary within such a definition.[25] Certainly the immigrant cases are adversary in character. The zeal [26] of the immigration inspectors to hunt down and exile the aliens, and the consequent loss to the latter of liberty, property, and ". . . all that makes life worth living"[27] makes these cases like criminal cases, though they are technically not such.[28] There is a social interest in having them fairly tried. It is difficult to escape the conclusions that they are not so tried, and that dispensing with the rules of evidence contributes to their unfairness.

Discrimination must be made between the commissions themselves. The proceedings of the Interstate Commerce Commission are clearly the most dependable.[29] Probably state public service commission hearings approach the same standard, except where there is denial of hearing by failure to introduce into the record, or to inform the parties and the reviewing courts of, evidence acted upon. Presumably the personnel of such commissions, and the fact that the parties are ordinarily represented by lawyers, is responsible. With certain exceptions the tax cases do not seem seriously unfair. Paradoxically, in the alien hearings where, because of the ignorance and helplessness of the aliens, and the serious consequences to them and their families of adverse decisions, there is great need of care and fairness, and more reason for strict application of the rules of evidence, there is much more laxity than in the

[24] In United States *v.* Abilene & S. R. Co., IV A *supra.*
[25] Chicago & Northwestern R. Co. *v.* Railroad Commission, lowering the rate on ice and awarding reparation, IV C *supra*; Spiller *v.* Atchison, Topeka & Santa Fe Ry., a reparation case, Montrose Oil Refining Co. *v.* St. Louis-San Francisco R. Co. which, in addition to making a rate reduction, awarded damages, United States *v.* Abilene & S. R. Co., a division of joint rates case, properly forbidding the use of data not introduced in evidence, and Beaumont, S. L. & W. R. Co. *v.* United States, a division of joint rates case, all IV A *supra.*
[26] "Ferocity" would be a better word in some instances. See *In re* Sugano, 40 F. (2d) 961 (Dist. Ct. Cal., 1930) and Whitfield *v.* Hanges, IV E *supra,* where, happily, the courts gave relief against the unfairness.
[27] Mr. Justice Brandeis in Ng Fung Ho *v.* White, 259 U. S. 276, 284 (1922).
[28] United States *ex rel.* Bilokumsky *v.* Tod, IV E 1 *supra.*
[29] The single case in the Federal Trade Commission warrants no comment.

Interstate Commerce Commission and state public service commission cases, where the effect of orders upon individuals is more remote and less serious.

The extreme view is not here urged that administrative hearings must be warped into the mold of judicial trials, or that the rules of evidence in full vigor are wholly appropriate thereto. Administrative justice, with its directness, its speed, its broad substantive standards [30] variably applicable "with time, place and circumstances,"[31] its problems calling for "common sense or the average moral judgment"[32] in the application of such standards, "rather than for deductive logic,"[33] is here, necessarily, and in its field, advantageously. Railroads must be extended, facilities improved, rates fixed, reparations paid, competitive rights made known, taxes collected. Even the immigrant cases demand speed. Thousands of the worthy come upon our gates. The unworthy must go.

Facts cannot always be found. Neither the laboratory nor the court finds all the facts; and even in courts controversies must end. Necessity drives us on. We act upon facts if we can, but without them if we must. Not all parties can have lawyers, and not all commissioners can be lawyers, to invoke and apply the rules of evidence for finding facts. Certain of the rules of evidence can be dispensed with as noted; and certain of the commissions, and certain of the commissions' functions, need them less than others. Moreover, it is hard to know how it would have been if it had been otherwise. It cannot with finality be demonstrated how differently the cases reviewed would have been decided had the rules of evidence been applied. Only by turning back time and events, and by re-trying the same cases before the same tribunals, but according to the rules of evidence, could this be known. All of this is conceded.

But while the old tools may not be wholly suited to the new tasks, they should, like the evidence before commissions, be used "for what they are worth," not thrown away. They may have some uses for which new tools, or no tools, are a poor substitute. The reaction against courts and their methods may be over severe. Characterization of the rules of evidence as "useless technical

---

[30] Note that in the alien cases there are narrow rules like those for criminal cases.

[31] Pound, *Jurisprudence, The History and Prospects of the Social Sciences* (1925), p. 474.

[32] *Ibid.*   [33] *Ibid.*

requirements," or as ceremonial obstacles to getting at the facts, indicates a failure to recognize that the "distillate of experience" may be wine as well as dregs, and that necessity, the common excuse for not taking pains, may be the mother of conjecture as well as of invention. It is submitted that even the expert commissioner should receive hearsay sparingly, should not deny himself the testing value of cross-examination, and should be willing to introduce what he acts upon.

The interests involved in the cases reviewed are important. In the alien cases the individual interest in freedom of opinion, of action, of choice of advantageous political, social and economic conditions and relations, and the social interest in the general security, health and morals are seen, as also the social interest in the individual interests mentioned; it has by legislative fiat been declared to be of social interest to admit aliens of socially suitable type. In the tax cases the individual and the public interest in substance are involved. In the Interstate Commerce Commission and public service commission cases the corporate and, through relation thereto, the individual interest in substance, and the social interest in convenience, adequacy, and economy of public service appear. Not to try such cases with care — to individualize them upon the adjective as well as upon the substantive side — is to recognize such interests in theory, only to impair or defeat them in practice. Legal acknowledgment of a right to remain in the United States is of little worth to the alien if he be deported upon carelessly accepted, and in his case false, hearsay. The social interest in cheap carriage will not be promoted if railroad values and service costs are not accurately found. Railroads will fail if rates are too low. Shippers will suffer if they are too high. There is a social interest in facts and in fairness. There is value in rules as well as in discretion.

APPENDICES

APPENDIX I

PUBLIC SERVICE COMMISSION STATUTES CONTAINING NO PROVISION CONCERNING THE RULES OF EVIDENCE

Connecticut. Conn. Gen. Stat. (1930), §§ 3577–3619 inclusive.

Indiana. Ind. Ann. Stat. (Burns, 1926), §§ 12,672–12,857 inclusive. Section 12,756 of the Indiana statutes provides: " . . . In all actions and proceedings *in court* [underlining the writer's] arising under this act, all processes shall be served and the practice and rules of evidence shall be the same as in civil actions, except as otherwise herein provided." This section is apparently intended to cover not evidence taken before the commission, but evidence in judicial proceedings on appeal from the commission. Thus, § 12,755 places the burden of proof in such proceedings on the party adverse to the commission. This Indiana provision is a common provision in many of the acts. See 1 Wigmore, *Evidence* (2d ed. 1923), § 4c, note 14, p. 44; and see Neb. Comp. Stat. (1929) 2c, 75, § 711, Ohio Gen. Code (Page, 1931), § 552, and Mich. Comp. Laws (1929), § 11,043. The exception in the Indiana statute apparently refers to § 12,748, of the same chapter, making rates in effect prima facie reasonable, § 12,752, providing that in actions in judicial tribunals on appeal from the commission, new evidence shall not be heard, but that the same shall be referred back to the commission, § 12,755, referred to *supra*, and § 12,757, concerning compulsory testimony and immunity.

Louisiana. La. Rev. Stat. Ann. (Marr, 1915), §§ 6127–6155 inclusive, "Railroad Commission."

Massachusetts. Mass. Gen. Laws (1921) c. 25, § 1–16 inclusive; and Acts of 1922, c. 259, § 1; 1923, c. 362, § 18, "Department of Public Utilities."

Mississippi. Miss. Code Ann. (1930), §§ 7023–7138 inclusive, "Railroad Commission."

South Carolina. S. C. Civ. Code (1932), §§ 8243–8292 inclusive, "Railroad Commission."

Washington. Wash. Comp. Stat. (Remington, 1922), §§ 10,339–10,459 inclusive, and Wash. Comp. Stat. (Remington, Supp. 1927), §§ 10,344–10,442 inclusive.

APPENDIX II

REFERENCES TO IMMIGRATION STATUTES EXAMINED

Chinese Exclusion Acts

July 28, 1868	16 Stat. 740
May 6, 1882	22 Stat. 58
July 5, 1884	23 Stat. 115
September 13, 1888	25 Stat. 476
October 1, 1888	25 Stat. 504
May 5, 1892	27 Stat. 25
March 17, 1894	28 Stat. 1210
April 29, 1902	32 Stat. 176
February 14, 1903	32 Stat. 828
April 27, 1904	33 Stat. 428
March 4, 1913	37 Stat. 737

Immigration Acts

Rev. Stat., Title XXIX, p. 378 (1874)	
March 3, 1875	18 Stat. 477
August 3, 1882	22 Stat. 214
June 26, 1884	23 Stat. 58
February 26, 1885	23 Stat. 332
February 23, 1887	24 Stat. 414
October 19, 1888	25 Stat. 566
March 3, 1891	26 Stat. 1084
February 15, 1893	27 Stat. 449
March 3, 1893	27 Stat. 569
August 18, 1894	28 Stat. 390
March 2, 1895	28 Stat. 780
June 6, 1900	31 Stat. 611
April 29, 1902	31 Stat. 176
March 3, 1903	32 Stat. 1213
February 14, 1903	32 Stat. 828
March 22, 1904	33 Stat. 144
April 28, 1904	33 Stat. 591
February 3, 1905	33 Stat. 684
February 6, 1905	33 Stat. 692
March 3, 1905	33 Stat. 1182
February 20, 1907	34 Stat. 898
March 2, 1907	34 Stat. 1228
March 4, 1909	35 Stat. 969
March 4, 1909	35 Stat. 1060
March 26, 1910	36 Stat. 763

APPENDIX II

June 25, 1910................... 36 Stat. 825
August 24, 1912................. 37 Stat. 476
March 4, 1913................... 37 Stat. 736
March 4, 1915................... 38 Stat. 1164, 1151
February 5, 1917................ 39 Stat. 874
May 9, 1918..................... 40 Stat. 545
May 22, 1918.................... 40 Stat. 559
October 16, 1918................ 40 Stat. 1012
October 19, 1918................ 40 Stat. 1014
May 10, 1920.................... 41 Stat. 593
June 5, 1920.................... 41 Stat. 981, 1008
December 26, 1920............... 41 Stat. 1082
May 19, 1921.................... 42 Stat. 5
May 11, 1922.................... 42 Stat. 540
May 26, 1922.................... 42 Stat. 596
June 30, 1922................... 42 Stat. 766
September 22, 1922.............. 42 Stat. 1021
December 27, 1922............... 42 Stat. 1065
May 26, 1924.................... 43 Stat. 153
May 28, 1924.................... 43 Stat. 240
June 2, 1924.................... 43 Stat. 253
June 7, 1924.................... 43 Stat. 669
February 27, 1925............... 43 Stat. 1049
May 20, 1926.................... 44 Stat. 568
May 26, 1926.................... 44 Stat. 654
May 26, 1926.................... 44 Stat. 657
July 3, 1926.................... 44 Stat. 812
March 4, 1927................... 44 Stat. 1415
March 4, 1927................... 44 Stat. 1455
March 31, 1928.................. 45 Stat. 400
April 2, 1928................... 45 Stat. 401
May 29, 1928.................... 45 Stat. 1009
January 19, 1929................ 45 Stat. 1089
January 25, 1929................ 45 Stat. 1094
March 2, 1929................... 45 Stat. 1495
March 2, 1929................... 45 Stat. 1508
March 2, 1929................... 45 Stat. 1512
March 4, 1929................... 45 Stat. 1551
June 24, 1929................... 46 Stat. 41
July 3, 1930.................... 46 Stat. 854
February 18, 1931............... 46 Stat. 1171
March 2, 1931................... 46 Stat. 1469

See, also, the *Administration of the Deportation Laws of the United States, a Report to the National Commission on Law Observance and Enforcement*, by Reuben Oppenheimer, especially pp. 32–40 inclusive, in Volume 2, parts 5–8, National Commission on Law Observance and Enforcement.

APPENDIX III

REFERENCES TO RULES EXAMINED

Alabama. 1927, Rules of Practice, C. C. H., P. U. and Carriers Service (1930), pp. 1505–1509.

Arkansas. 1901, Rules of Practice before the Commission, First Annual Report of Railroad Commission, p. 47.

Arizona. 1913, Rules of Practice and Procedure, Arizona Corporation Commission.

California. 1929, Rules of Procedure of the Railroad Commission, C. C. H., P. U. and Carriers Service (1930), pp. 1501–1508b.

Colorado. 1919, Rules of Procedure of the Public Utility Commission.

District of Columbia. Rules of Procedure adopted December 1, 1915 and amended December 19, 1927; see also Rules for Conduct of Hearing in Case No. 205.

Federal Trade Commission. 1913, Rules of Practice, Annual Report, Federal Trade Commission for Fiscal Year Ended June 30, 1931, pp. 148–151.

Hawaii. 1920, Rules of Practice and Procedure of the Public Utilities Commission.

Idaho. 1918, Rules of Practice and Procedure of the Public Utilities Commission of the State of Idaho.

Illinois. 1917, Rules of Practice and Procedure, C. C. H., P. U. and Carriers Service (1930), pp. 606–608.

Interstate Commerce Commission. 1930, Rules of Practice, Interstate Commerce Acts, Ann., pp. 3437–3505.

Iowa. 1911, Rules of Practice, Report of Railroad Commissioners, 1912, p. 225, C. C. H., P. U. and Carriers Service (1931), pp. 1507–1509.

Kentucky. 1931, Rules of Practice Before the Railroad Commission of Kentucky.

Louisiana. 1929, Rules and Regulations of the Louisiana Public Utility Service Commission, Ninth Annual Report, p. 9.

Maine. 1926, Rules of Practice and Procedure, Public Utilities Commission of Maine.

Maryland. 1918, Rules of Practice and Procedure of the Public Service Commission, Reports of Public Service Commission, Vol. I, p. 180, C. C. H., P. U. and Carriers Service (1931), pp. 1521–1529.

APPENDIX III

Michigan. 1920, Rules of Practice before the Commission, C. C. H., P. U. and Carriers Service (1930), pp. 1501–1508.

Missouri. 1913, Rules of Practice and Procedure, C. C. H., P. U. and Carriers Service (1930), pp. 1501–1511.

Nebraska. 1908, Rules of Practice, First Annual Report of Nebraska State Railway Commission, p. 467.

Nevada. 1923, Rules of Practice before the Public Service Commission.

New Hampshire. 1932, Rules of Procedure and Regulations Covering Matters before the Public Service Commission.

New Jersey. Rules of the Board of Public Utility Commissioners, Public Utility Commissioners' Report (1911), p. 469, C. C. H., P. U. and Carriers Service (1930), pp. 1509–1511.

New Mexico. 1913, Additional Rules of Procedure of State Corporation Commission.

New York. 1928, Rules of Practice of the Department of Public Service, State Division, C. C. H., P. U. and Carriers Service (1930), pp. 1001–1009.

North Carolina. 1931, Rules of Practice and Procedure of the North Carolina Corporation Commission.

Ohio. 1932, Rules of Practice before the Utilities Commission of Ohio, C. C. H., P. U. and Carriers Service (1930), pp. 1501–1504.

Oklahoma. 1915, Rules of Practice, C. C. H., P. U. and Carriers Service (1931), p. 1515.

Oregon. 1913, Rules of Practice and Procedure before the Public Service Commission, C. C. H., P. U. and Carriers Service (1931), pp. 1511–1515.

Pennsylvania. 1931, Rules of Practice before the Public Service Commission of the Commonwealth of Pennsylvania, C. C. H., P. U. and Carriers Service (1930), pp. 601–606A.

Rhode Island. Rules of Practice and Procedure, Report of Public Utility Commission, 1912, p. 69.

Porto Rico. 1917, Rules and Regulations of the Public Service Commission of Porto Rico.

South Carolina. 1931, Rules of Practice and Procedure.

Tennessee. 1919, amended 1921, Rules and Regulations Promulgated by Railroad and Public Utilities Commission, General Rules, p. 20.

Texas. Rules of Practice, C. C. H., P. U. and Carriers Service (1930), p. 1507.

Utah. 1917, Rules of Practice and Procedure of the Public Utilities Commission of Utah.

APPENDIX III

Virginia. 1924, Rules of Practice and Procedure in Cases and Proceedings before the State Corporation Commission.

Washington. 1929, Practice and Procedure before the Department of Public Works of Washington.

West Virginia. 1931, Rules of Practice and Procedure.

Wisconsin. 1906, Rules of Practice, First Biennial Report of the Railroad Commission, p. 926, C. C. H., P. U. and Carriers Service (1931), pp. 1502–1502d.

TABLE OF AUTHORITIES

TABLE OF AUTHORITIES

Cases

Atchison, T. & S. F. R. Co. v. Public Service Commission of Kansas,
   130 Kansas 777, 288 P. 755 (1930).......... 40, 44, 45, 87, 97, 100

Beaumont, S. L. & W. R. Co. v. United States, 36 F. (2d) 789 (1929)
   aff'd. 282 U. S. 74 (1930)................ 27, 28, 29, 30, 34, 87, 101
Brader v. Zurbrick, 38 F. (2d) 472 (C. C. A. 6th, 1930)........... 56, 67
Brewer v. Railroad Commission, 190 Cal. 60, 210 P. 511 (1922)..... 38
Browne v. Zurbrick, 45 F. (2d) 931, 932 (C. C. A. 6th, 1930)....... 96

Cahan v. Carr, 47 F. (2d) 604 (C. C. A. 9th, 1931)........ 58, 67, 87
Caranica v. Nagle, 23 F. (2d) 545 (C. C. A. 9th, 1928)........ 57, 58, 67
Chicago & Northwestern R. Co. v. Railroad Commission, 156 Wisc.
   47, 145 N. W. 974 (1914)...... 33, 34, 35, 44, 45, 86, 87, 96, 98, 101
Chin Ah Yoke v. White, 244 Fed. 940 (C. C. A. 9th, 1917)..... 57, 67, 96
Chin Shee v. White, 273 Fed. 801 (C. C. A. 9th, 1921)   63, 64, 65, 67, 87, 99
Chin Yow v. United States, 208 U. S. 8 (1908) 54
Choy Gum v. Backus, 223 Fed. 487 (C. C. A. 9th, 1915).......... 64
City of Huntington et al. v. Public Serv. Commission, 101 W. Va.
   378, 133 S. E. 144 (1926)................................... 43
City of Norwalk v. Connecticut Co., 88 Conn. 471 (1914)....... 33, 44
Consolidated Southwestern Cases, 123 I. C. C. 203 (1927)........ 28

Duluth Street R. Co. v. Railroad Commission, 161 Wisc. 245, 152
   N. W. 887 (1915)................... 33, 35, 36, 44, 45, 87, 95, 96, 99

Eager v. Pub. Util. Comm., 113 O. St. 605, 149 N. E. 865 (1925)... 41
Ex Parte Cahan 42 F. (2d) 664 (Dist. Ct. Cal., 1930)............ 58
Ex Parte Garcia, 205 Fed. 53 (Dist. Ct. Cal., 1913)............. 64, 67
Ex Parte Jurgans, 17 F. (2d) 507 (Dist. Ct. Minn., 1927)......... 66
Ex Parte Mouratis, 21 F. (2d) 694 (Dist. Ct. Cal., 1927).........64, 67
Ex Parte Zavala, 298 Fed. 544 (Dist. Ct. Texas, 1924)........... 64

Ghiggeri v. Nagle, 19 F. (2d) 875 (C. C. A. 9th, 1927)............ 64, 67
Grubb v. Public Utilities Commission, 119 O. St. 264, 163 N. E. 713
   (1928)... 39, 45

Healy v. Backus, 221 Fed. 358 (C. C. A. 9th, 1915)........ 60, 61, 67
Hoffman v. Pub. Serv. Comm., 99 Pa. Super. Ct. 417 (1930).. 42, 43, 45
Hopson's Appeal, 65 Conn. 140, 31 Atl. 531 (1894).............. 33

In re Sugano, 40 F. (2d) 961 (Dist. Ct. Cal., 1930).............. 101

116   TABLE OF AUTHORITIES

Interstate Commerce Commission *v.* Baird, 194 U. S. 25 (1904)
        20, 21, 22, 23, 25, 30, 31, 44, 55, 58, 86
Interstate Commerce Commission *v.* Louisville & N. R. Co., 227 U. S.
 88 (1912)......... 21, 22, 23, 24, 25, 28, 30, 31, 32, 36, 40, 54, 86, 97

Jeung Bow *v.* United States, 228 Fed. 868 (C. C. A. 2d, 1915)...... 59
John Bene & Sons, Inc. *v.* Federal Trade Commission, 299 Fed. 468
 (C. C. A. 2d, 1924).............................. 31, 32, 82, 87
Johnson *v.* Kock Shing, 3 F. (2d) 889 (C. C. A. 1st, 1915)..... 55, 62, 67
Jung See *v.* Nash, 4 F. (2d) 639 (C. C. A. 8th, 1925) 55, 67

Kwock Jan Fat *v.* White, 253 U. S. 454 (1920).............. 54, 58, 97

Lake Co. *v.* Laconia, 68 N. H. 284, 35 Atl. 252 (1895).......... 46, 51
Lee Lung *v.* Patterson, 186 U. S. 168 (1902)..................... 57
Lee Sim *v.* United States, 218 Fed. 432 (C. C. A. 2d, 1914)..... 59, 67
Lewis *ex rel.* Lai Thuey Lem *v.* Johnson, 16 F. (2d) 180 (C. C. A. 1st,
 1926)... 66
Lindsey *v.* Pub. Util. Comm., 111 O. St. 6, 144 N. E. 729 (1924) 39, 45, 87
Lowell *v.* Commissioners of Middlesex County, 152 Mass. 372, 25
 N. E. 469, second case (1890)........................ 46, 50, 51
Lucas *v.* Brooks, 18 Wall. 436 (1873) 59
Lydston *v.* Rockingham County Light & Power Co., 75 N. H. 23,
 70 A. 385, 21 Ann. Cas. 1236 (1908) 55

Montrose Oil Refining Co. *v.* St. Louis-San Francisco R. Co., 25 F.
 (2d) 750 (1927) aff'd. 755 (C. C. A. 5th, 1928) certiorari denied
 277 U. S. 598 (1928).......................... 26, 27, 30, 87, 101
Moy Said Ching *v.* Tillinghast, 21 F. (2d) 810 (C. C. A. 1st, 1927).. 55, 67
Moy Yoke Shue *v.* Johnson, 290 Fed. 621 (Dist. Ct. Mass., 1923)
               61, 62, 67, 87

New England Divisions Case, 261 U. S. 184 (1923)..............25, 30
Newhall *v.* Jenkins, 2 Gray 562 (1854) 54
Ng Fung Ho *v.* White, 259 U. S. 276 (1922) 101
Ng Mon Tong *v.* Weedin, 43 F. (2d) 718 (C. C. A. 9th, 1930) 63
Norfolk and W. R. Co. *v.* Tidewater R. Co., 105 Va. 129, 52 S. E.
 852 (1906)... 14
Northern Pacific Ry. Co. *v.* Department of Public Works, 268 U. S.
 39 (1925).. 45

Ohio Valley Water Co. *v.* Ben Avon Borough, 253 U. S. 287 (1920) . 37

Pennsylvania R. Co. *v.* United States, 40 F. (2d) 921 (Dist. Ct.
 Pa., 1930) 29, 30, 37
People *v.* Hicks, 105 N. Y. 198, 11 N. E. 653 (Court of Appeals of
 N. Y., 1887)....................................... 47, 51, 86, 87
People *v.* Public Service Commission of Second Dist. of New York,
 127 App. Div. 480, 112 N. Y. Supp. 133 (1908).............. 44

TABLE OF AUTHORITIES 117

People *ex rel.* American Mfg. Co. *v.* Gifford, 134 Misc. 487, 235 N. Y.
   Supp. 578 (1929)... 50
People *ex rel.* Empire Mortgage Co. *v.* Cantor, 190 App. Div. 512,
   180 N. Y. Supp. 139 (1920).............................. 50, 51
People *ex rel.* Haile *v.* Brundage, 195 App. Div. 745, 187 N. Y. Supp.
   460 (1921).. 50
People *ex rel.* Hunt *v.* Priest, 90 App. Div. 520, 85 N. Y. Supp. 481
   (1904)... 49, 50, 51, 87
People *ex rel.* Schabacker *v.* State Assessors, 47 Hun 450 (N. Y. 1888)
                                                  48, 49, 50, 51, 86, 87
People *ex rel.* The Board of Supervisors of Chenango Co. *v.* The Board
   of State Assessors, 22 Weekly Dig. 453, N. Y. Sup. Court (1885)   49
Pratt *v.* Raymond, 188 Ill. 469, 58 N. E. 16 (1900)......... 46, 51, 96, 99

St. Louis Southwestern Ry. Co. *v.* Stewart, 150 Ark. 586, 235 S. W.
   1003 (1921)....................................... 37, 45, 87, 100
Schuylkill Ry. Co. *v.* Pub. Service Comm., 268 Pa. 430, 112 Atl. 5
   (1920) aff'g. 71 Pa. Super. Ct. 204 .... 41, 42, 43, 44, 45, 46, 87
Soo Hoo Do Yim *v.* Tillinghast, 24 F. (2d) 163 (C. C. A. 1st, 1928).   66
Spiller *v.* Atchison, Topeka & Santa Fe Ry., 253 U. S. 117 (1920)
                                              22, 23, 24, 25, 30, 87, 101
Steamboat Canal Co. *v.* Garson, 43 Nev. 298, 185 P. 801 (1919)
                                              36, 37, 43, 44, 45, 86, 96
Steenerson *v.* Great Northern Ry. Co., 69 Minn. 353, 72 N. W. 713
   (1897)... 32, 33, 44, 86, 99

Tagg Bros. & Moorehead *v.* United States, 280 U. S. 420 (1930)...   43
Tang Tun *v.* Edsell, 223 U. S. 673 (1912)............. 54, 64, 65, 66, 87

United States *v.* Abilene & S. R. Co., 265 U. S. 274 (1924)
                                24, 25, 26, 28, 30, 31, 32, 34, 35, 97, 101
United States *v.* B. & O. Southwestern Ry., 226 U. S. 14 (1912) ..   43
United States *v.* Curran, 4 F. (2d) 356 (C. C. A. 3d, 1925)........   66
United States *v.* Hughes, 299 Fed. 99 (C. C. A. 3d, 1924)...... 56, 57, 67
United States *v.* Uhl, 215 Fed. 573 (C. C. A. 2d, 1914).... 59, 60, 67, 87
United States *v.* Uhl, 266 Fed. 34 (C. C. A. 2d, 1920)............   64
United States *ex rel.* Bilokumsky *v.* Tod, 263 U. S. 149 (1923)
                                              25, 54, 59, 63, 66, 91, 101
United States *ex rel.* Fong On *v.* Day, 39 F. (2d) 202 (Dist. Ct. N. Y.
   1930).. 63
United States *ex rel.* Ng Wing *v.* Brough, 15 F. (2d) 377 (C. C. A. 2d,
   1926)... 62, 67, 87, 96, 97
United States *ex rel.* Smith *v.* Curran, 12 F. (2d) 636 (C. C. A. 2d,
   1926).. 62, 96
United States *ex rel.* Tomasso *v.* Flynn, 22 F. (2d) 174 (Dist. Ct. N. Y.
   1927).. 57, 67

Western Paper Makers' Chemical Co. *v.* United States, 271 U. S. 268
   (1926)....................................... 25, 26, 27, 30, 87

TABLE OF AUTHORITIES

Western Union Tel. Co. *v.* Dodge County, 80 Neb. 18, 113 N. W. 805
(1907)... 47, 50, 51, 87
White *v.* Chan Wy Sheung, 270 Fed. 765 (C. C. A. 9th, 1921) 61, 96
Whitfield *v.* Hanges, 222 Fed. 745 (C. C. A. 9th, 1915)...... 58, 97, 101
Wichita R. & Light Co. *v.* Court of Industrial Relations, 113 Kansas
217, 214 P. 797 (1923)................................... 40, 41, 98
Williamson *v.* Railroad Commission, 193 Cal. 22, 222 P. 803 (1924)
37, 38, 44, 45

Yip Wah *v.* Nagle, 7 F. (2d) 426 (C. C. A. 9th, 1925) 63

TREATISES

Dickinson: Administrative Justice and the Supremacy of Law
(1927), p. 35... 3
Freund: Administrative Powers over Persons and Property (1928),
p. 169, s. 83... 4
Henderson: Federal Trade Commission (1924), p. 64............ 3, 83
Jones: Evidence (2d ed.), s. 589.............................. 57
Wigmore: Evidence (2d ed., 1923), s. 4b, p. 27................. 3
Wigmore: Evidence (2d ed., 1923), s. 4b, p. 28................. 3
Wigmore: Evidence (2d ed., 1923), s. 194, pp. 417, 418.......... 57

ESSAYS

Pound: The Administrative Application of Legal Standards, XLIV
A. B. A. Rep. (1919), p. 445............................... 4
Pound: Jurisprudence, The History and Prospects of the Social Sciences (1925), p. 474...................................... 102
Pound: The Revival of Personal Government, New Hampshire
Bar Association Proceedings (1917), pp. 13, 33............... 4
Ross: Applicability of Common Law Rules of Evidence in Proceedings before Workmen's Compensation Commissions (1923), 36
Harv. L. Rev. 263.. 4

CASEBOOKS

Frankfurter and Davison: Cases on Administrative Law (1932),
Preface, p. vii... 4

MISCELLANEOUS

II Bouvier: Law Dictionary, Rawle's Revision (1897), 866 21
Reuben Oppenheimer: Administration of the Deportation Laws of
the United States, A Report to the National Commission on Law
Observance and Enforcement, Vol. 2, parts 5–8, National Commission on Law Observance and Enforcement (1931) 51
Vol. 6, Records and Briefs for 282 U. S. Sup. Ct. Reports, and therein
p. 92 *et seq.* of Appellant's Brief and p. 46 *et seq.* of Brief for the
Interstate Commerce Commission.......................... 28

TABLE OF AUTHORITIES 119

Vol. 5, Records and Briefs, U. S. C .C .A., Fifth Circuit, 25 F. (2d), pp. 76 and 77 of Brief for the Plaintiffs in Error together with references to the Transcript of Record therein made.......... 26
Vol. 18, Cases and Points for 253 U. S. Supreme Court Reports, p. 392 of the Transcript of Record and p. 12 *et seq.*, 26 *et seq.*, 42 *et seq.*, and 49 *et seq.* of Brief for Defendants in Error and pp. 233 to 282 inclusive of the Transcript of Record................. 24
Vol. 24, Records and Briefs for 271 U. S. Supreme Court Reports, pp. 19 and 30 of Plaintiffs' Brief, pp. 12 and 13 of Brief for Interstate Commerce Commission, pp. 140–141 of Transcript of Record.. 26
Twenty-second Annual Report of the I. C. C. (1908), p. 10....... 82

STATUTES

24 Stat. 383 (1887), 49 U. S. C. § 12 (1) (1926)................. 7
24 Stat. 383, 384 (1887), 49 U. S. C. § 13 (1) (1926)............. 8
24 Stat. 385 (1887), 49 U. S. C. § 17 (1) (1926)................. 8
24 Stat. 386 (1887), 49 U. S. C. § 19 (2) (1926)................. 7
25 Stat. 858, 859 (1889), 49 U. S. C. § 12 (1) (1926)............. 7
26 Stat. 743 (1891), 49 U. S. C. § 12 (2) (1926)................. 7
26 Stat. 743, 744 (1891), 49 U. S. C. § 12 (4) (1926)............. 7
26 Stat. 743, 744 (1891), 49 U. S. C. § 12 (5) (1926)............. 8
34 Stat. 594, 595 (1906), 49 U. S. C. § 20 (10) (1926)............ 8
36 Stat. 550 (1910), 49 U. S. C. § 13 (2) (1926)................. 8
37 Stat. 701 (1913), 49 U. S. C. § 19a (c) (1926)................ 8
38 Stat. 717–724 (1914), 15 U. S. C. §§ 41–51 (1926)............. 8
40 Stat. 270 (1917), 49 U. S. C. § 17 (1) (1926)................. 8
Ala. Code (Michie, 1928), §§ 9621, 9667, 9802................... 10
Ariz. Code (Struckmeyer, 1928), § 709......................... 10
Ark. Dig. Stat. (Crawford and Moses, 1921), § 1683............. 11
Cal. Gen. Laws (Deering, 1923) Act 6386, § 53.................. 11
Col. Ann. Stat. (Mills, 1930), § 5933L......................... 11
D. C. Code (1929), tit. 26, § 54............................... 9
Fla. Comp. Laws (1927), § 6738................................ 13
Ga. Code Ann. (Michie, 1926), §§ 2626, 2636, 2637, 2641......... 13
Hawaii Rev. Laws (1925) § 2200................................ 11
Idaho Comp. Stat. (1919), § 2478.............................. 11
Ill. Rev. Stat. (Cahill, 1931), c. 111a, §§ 23 and 79............. 11, 47
Iowa Code (1931), § 7867...................................... 12
Kansas Rev. Stat. Ann. (1923), c. 66, § 106.................... 9
Ky. Stat. (Carroll, 1930), § 201e–14, § 201e–22................. 13
Me. Rev. Stat. (1930), c. 62, §§ 59, 66, 67, 68................. 13, 14
Md. Ann. Code (Bagby, 1924), art. 23, § 358.................... 11
Mich. Comp. Laws (1929) § 11018............................... 9
Minn. Stat. (Mason, 1927), § 4636............................. 12
Mo. Rev. Stat. (1929), § 5144................................. 12
Mont. Rev. Codes (Choate, 1921) § 3894........................ 9
Neb. Comp. Stat. (1929), c. 75, § 301.......................... 9
Nev. Comp. Laws (Hillyer, 1929) § 6105........................ 10

TABLE OF AUTHORITIES

N. H. Pub. Laws (1926) c. 238, §§ 9 and 10	12
N. J. Comp. Stat. (Supp. 1924), p. 2893, § 167–46	12
N. M. Stat. Ann. (Courtright, 1929), § 134–1120	10
N. Y. Code of Civil Procedure (1887) § 2140, subd. 3	49
N. Y. Cons. Laws (Cahill, 1930) c. 49 § 20 — N. Y. Pub. Serv. Comm. Law (1910)	12
N. Y. Laws of 1876, c. 49	48
N. C. Code Ann. (Michie, 1931) § 1093	14
N. D. Comp. Laws Ann. (Supp. 1925) § 4609c24	12
Ohio Gen. Code (Page, 1932) § 499–6	9
Ohio Gen. Code (1921) §§ 499–8–11–15 and 614–6	39
Okla. Comp. Stat. Ann. (Bunn, 1921), §§ 3487, 3488	13
Comp. Okla. Stat. Ann. (Supp. Thornton, 1926), §§ 5459–5, 5459–6	13
Oregon Code Ann. (1930), § 61–110	9
Pa. Stat. Ann. (Purdon, 1930), tit. 66, § 711	9
R. I. Gen. Laws (1923) c. 253, § 17	12
S. D. Comp. Laws (1929) § 9497	9
Tenn. Code (1932) § 5399	9
Texas Rev. Civ. Code (Vernon, 1928) art. 6450	9
Utah Comp. Laws (1917) § 4820	12
Vt. Gen. Laws (1917) § 5036	9
Va. Code of 1904, Acts 1902–03–04, pp. 137, 143	14
Va. Code Ann. (Michie, 1930) § 3723	14
W. Va. Code (1931) c. 24, art. I, § 7	12
Wis. Stat. (1931), § 195.03 (1) (5)	10
Wyoming Rev. Stat. (Courtright, 1931), §§ 94–150, 94–162	9, 82

Rules

Rule XIII (a), (b), (c), (g), and (h), Rules of Practice of the Interstate Commerce Commission, 1930	16, 86
Rules IX, XIII, and XIV, Rules of Practice of the Federal Trade Commission, 1913	16, 86
Rule XI (h), Rules of Procedure of the Public Utilities Commission of the District of Columbia, 1929	17
Rule 7, Rules of Practice and Procedure of the Illinois Commerce Commission, C. C. H., P. U. and Carriers Service, 1930	17, 86
Rule XI (b), Rules of Practice of the Board of Railroad Commissioners of Iowa, 1912	18, 86
Rule IX, Rules of Practice and Procedure, Public Utilities Commission of Maine, 1926	18, 86
Rule II, Additional Rules of Procedure of State Corporation Commission of New Mexico, 1913	18, 86
Rule XI, Practice and Procedure before Department of Public Works of Washington, 1929	18, 81, 86
Rule 19, D, 1, Immigration Laws and Rules of January 1, 1930	18, 86
Rule 12, B, 1, Rule 23, Rule 12, C, 1, Rule 12, C, 2 and Rule 24, A, 1, Immigration Laws and Rules of January 1, 1930	19, 86

INDEX

INDEX

Adjective law, individualization of, 103
Administrative justice, advantages of, 102
Administrative law, in operation, desirability of study of, 4
Adversary
　methods of trial, 96
　proceedings, 100–101
Alabama
　legislation, 10
Alaska, 14
Alien exclusion and deportation hearings, 4, 15, 18–19, 51–67
　effect upon of dispensing with rules of evidence, 101–102
　fairness, 54, 56, 57, 58, 59, 63–64, 65, 66
　interests involved in, 103
　judicial decisions concerning, 51–67
　resumé of statutes and procedure, 51–54
　rules infringed in, 89–90
　rules of evidence in
　　conclusions, 56
　　denial of cross-examination, 57–58
　　former conviction, 57
　　general rule, 53–55
　　hearsay, 59–66
　　immateriality, 56–57
　　impeachment, 55–56
　　oath, 59
　　testimony of wife against husband, 58–59
　summary of judicial decisions concerning, 66–67
　types of evidence admitted in, 90
　unfairness of, 101
Arizona
　legislation, 10–11
　practice in commission, 68–69

Arkansas
　judicial decisions, *see* Table of Cases
　legislation, 11
　practice in commission, 69

Brandeis, Mr. Justice, quoted, 25, 26, 30, 53–54, 100–101
　on rules of evidence in deportation hearings, 53–54

California
　judicial decisions, *see* Table of Cases
　legislation, 11
Colorado
　legislation, 11
　practice in commission, 69
Commission hearings, dependability of, 101–102
Commissioners
　expertness of, 32–33, 35, 93–94, 95
　not to be arbitrary, 49, 51
　personal information of, 30–31, 90, 97, 99
　view by, 37, 45, 98
Commissions
　relation of kinds of work of to rules of evidence, 99–100
Conclusions, 56, 92–103
Connecticut
　judicial decisions, *see* Table of Cases
　legislation, 14
　practice in commission, 69
Courts and commissions' reasons for not applying rules of evidence, 89
Cross-examination
　denial of, 57–58, 62, 64, 67, 91, 95–96
　required, 39, 45
　value of, 96

Delaware, 14
Dickinson, John, quoted, 3
District of Columbia
  legislation, 9
  practice in commission, 69–70
  rules, 17
Due process, 54, 61, 66, 67

Evidence
  acted upon but not introduced, 98–99
  affidavits as, 48–49, 57, 64
  competent, 41, 45, 48, 49
  dependability, sacrifice of, 6
  effect of non-introduction upon review, 98
  essential rules preserved, 22, 31
  hearsay, 23, 30, 31, 32, 34–35, 36–49, 51, 59–67
  immaterial, 32, 56–57, 67
  impeaching as affirmative proof, 55–56
  incompetent, 24, 25, 30, 58, 59, 67
  introduction required, 30–31
  irrelevant, 45
  necessity of legal, 38, 45
  necessity of public presentation, 40, 45
  not introduced, 25, 30, 31, 32, 35–36, 37, 39–40, 42–43, 44–45, 47–48, 90–91, 97
  obtained in secrecy, 46–47, 51, 90–91, 99
  official records, 64–66
  opinion, 31–32, 40–41, 45, 46, 50, 51, 56, 67
  opportunity to examine, 39, 45
  personal information as, 30–31, 45, 97
  records in other proceedings, 64–66
  relevant, 21, 30–31, 44
  secondary, 31–32, 41–42, 46
  typical, 30
  view and personal information, 98

Facts, difficulty of finding, 102
Federal Trade Commission, 3–4
  judicial decisions, 31–32
  legislation, 8–9
  practice in, 82, 83
  rules, 16
  rules of evidence infringed by, 89, 90
  types of evidence admitted by, 90
Florida
  legislation, 13
Former conviction, 57
Frankfurter, Felix, and Davidson, J. Forrester, on empirical state of administrative law, 4
Freund, Ernst, 4

Gardner, circuit judge, quoted, 27
Georgia
  legislation, 13
  practice in commission, 70

Hawaii
  legislation, 11
  practice in commission, 70–71
Hearing
  de novo, effect of, 36, 37, 40–41, 44, 45, 87
  denial of, 97–99
  fairness of, 67
Hearsay, 59–66
  introduced through hearsay, 62
Henderson, Girard C., quoted, 3–4
Holmes, Mr. Justice, quoted, 60

Idaho
  legislation, 11
Illinois
  judicial decisions, *see* Table of Cases
  legislation, 11
  practice in commission, 71–72
  rules, 17
Immateriality, 56, 57
Immigration tribunals
  denial of right of cross-examination in, 91
  rules of evidence infringed by, 89–90
  types of evidence admitted by, 90
Impeachment, 55–56, 67
Indiana
  legislation, 14
  practice in commission, 72

INDEX

Individualization, 4–5, 103
Interests, and impairment of, 103
Interstate Commerce Commission, 4
  dependability of hearings in, 101
  evidence
    freedom of commission respecting rules of, 7–8
    not introduced, 90
    rules of infringed by commission, 89–90
    types of admitted, 90
  interests involved in cases in, 103
  judicial decisions, 20–31
    summary, 30–31
  legislation, 7–8
  personal information of commissioners, 90
  practice in, 82
  rules, 16
Iowa
  legislation, 12
  practice in commission, 72
  rules, 17–18

Judgments, 67
Judicial decisions, 20–67
  alien exclusion and deportation, 51–67, summary, 66–67
  Federal Trade Commission, 31–32
  in particular states, see Table of Cases
  Interstate Commerce Commission, 20–31, summary, 30–31
  state public service commissions, 32–46, summary, 44–46
  taxation, 46–51, summary, 50–51

Kansas
  judicial decisions, see Table of Cases
  legislation, 9
Kentucky
  legislation, 13

Lamar, Mr. Justice, quoted, 97
Legislation, 7–15
  Federal Trade Commission, 8–9
  Interstate Commerce Commission, 7–8

  state public service commissions, 9–14
  summaries and comparisons, 85–86
  United States Bureau of Immigration, 15
Louisiana
  legislation, 14
  practice in commission, 72

Maine
  legislation, 13–14
  practice in commission, 72–73
  rules, 18
Maryland
  legislation, 11
  practice in commission, 73
Massachusetts
  judicial decisions, see Table of Cases
  legislation, 14
  practice in commission, 73
Materials covered, 5–6
Michigan
  legislation, 9
Minnesota
  judicial decisions, see Table of Cases
  legislation, 12–13
  practice in commission, 73
Mississippi
  legislation, 14
Missouri
  legislation, 12
  practice in commission, 73–75
Montana
  legislation, 9

National Commission on Law Observance and Enforcement, Report to, on administration of deportation laws, Reuben Oppenheimer, 51–54
Nebraska
  judicial decisions, see Table of Cases
  legislation, 9
  practice in commission, 75
Nevada
  judicial decisions, see Table of Cases

INDEX

Nevada (*continued*)
  legislation, 10
  practice in commission, 75
New Hampshire
  judicial decisions, *see* Table of Cases
  legislation, 12
New Jersey
  legislation, 12
  practice in commission, 75
New Mexico
  legislation, 10
  practice in commission, 76
  rules, 18
New York
  judicial decisions, *see* Table of Cases
  legislation, 12
  practice in commission, 76–77
North Carolina
  legislation, 14
  practice in commission, 77–78
North Dakota
  legislation, 12

Oath, 7–8, 46, 50, 51, 59, 67, 96
Objections, manner of taking, 24
Ohio
  judicial decisions, *see* Table of Cases
  legislation, 9
  practice in commission, 78
Oklahoma
  legislation, 13
  practice in commission, 78–79
Oppenheimer, Reuben, *Administration of the Deportation Laws of the United States*, 51–54
Oregon
  legislation, 9

Pennsylvania
  judicial decisions, *see* Table of Cases
  legislation, 9
  practice in commission, 79
Pitney, Mr. Justice, quoted, 23

Pound, Roscoe
  on administrative justice, 102
  on duty of jurists concerning administrative law, 4
Practice in the commissions, 68–84
  Arizona, 68–69
  Arkansas, 69
  Colorado, 69
  Connecticut, 69
  District of Columbia, 69–70
  Federal Trade Commission, 82
  Georgia, 70
  Hawaii, 70–71
  Illinois, 71–72
  Indiana, 72
  Interstate Commerce Commission, 82
  Iowa, 72
  Louisiana, 72
  Maine, 72–73
  Maryland, 73
  Massachusetts, 73
  Minnesota, 73
  Missouri, 73–75
  Nebraska, 75
  Nevada, 75
  New Jersey, 75
  New Mexico, 76
  New York, 76–77
  North Carolina, 77–78
  Ohio, 78
  Oklahoma, 78–79
  Pennsylvania, 79
  questionnaire concerning, 68
  Rhode Island, 79
  South Carolina, 79
  summaries and comparisons, 87–89
  summary concerning, 82–84
  Tennessee, 79–80
  Texas, 80
  Utah, 80–81
  Vermont, 81
  Virginia, 81
  Washington, 81
  West Virginia, 81
  Wyoming, 81–82

Rhode Island
  legislation, 12

INDEX

Rhode Island (*continued*)
  practice in commission, 79
Ross, Frank A., 4
Rules, 16–19
  examined, 16
  Federal Trade Commission, 16
  Interstate Commerce Commission, 16
  state public service commissions, 16–18
  summaries and comparisons, 86
  United States Bureau of Immigration, 18–19
Rules of evidence
  applicability of to administrative hearings, 3
  applicability of in different kinds of commission work, 99–100
  applied by business men, 94
  avoidance of regardless of facts, 95
  commission rules concerning, 16–19
  discriminations as to applying, 95
  effect upon court trials of non-application of, 94
  in rate cases, 100
  infringed, 90
  judicial decisions concerning, *see* Judicial decisions
  kinds of discussed, 5–6
  non-application of, how far warranted, 94–103
  not applied, 92–93
  obligation to preserve essential rules, 97
  popular view of, 3, 92
  reasons for not applying, 93–94
  relaxation of and denial of hearing, 97–99
  statutory provisions concerning, 7–15
  "technical," 21, 30, 33, 44, 92
    commission rule against, 17
    statutory strictures upon, 10–12
  types of matter received in violation of, 30, 31, 32, 45, 51, 67, 90
  use of required by statute, 13–14
  usefulness of, 3, 94
  where commission work legislative or supervisory, 100

Science of law, 4–5
Smith, Mr. Justice, quoted, 49
South Carolina
  legislation, 14
  practice in commission, 79
South Dakota
  legislation, 9–10
State public service commissions, 4
  dependability of hearings in, 101
  interests involved in cases in, 103
  judicial decisions, 32–46
  legislation, 9–14
  non-introduction of evidence in hearings in, 90–91
  rules, 16–18
  rules of evidence infringed by, 89, 90
  summary of judicial decisions concerning, 44–46
  types of evidence admitted by, 90
States, judicial decisions in particular states, *see* Table of Cases
Statutes, *see* Legislation
Summaries and comparisons, 85–91
  courts and commissions' reasons for not applying rules of evidence, 89
  judicial decisions, 86–87, 89–91
  legislation, 85–86
  practice in the commissions, 87–89
  rules, 86

Taxation
  assessment, abatement, and equalization tribunals, 4
    rules of evidence infringed by, 89–90
    secret evidence in, 90–91
    types of evidence admitted by, 90
  hearings
    fairness of, 101
    interests involved in, 103
    judicial decisions, 46–50, summary, 50–51
Tennessee
  legislation, 9
  practice in commission, 79–80
Testimony, of wife against husband, 58–59, 67

INDEX

Texas
  legislation, 9
  practice in commission, 80

United States Bureau of Immigration
  legislation, 15
  rules, 18–19

Utah
  legislation, 12
  practice in commission, 80–81

Vermont
  legislation, 9
  practice in commission, 81

Virginia
  judicial decisions, *see* Table of Cases
  legislation, 14
  practice in commission, 81

Washington
  legislation, 14
  practice in commission, 81
  rules, 18

West Virginia
  judicial decisions, *see* Table of Cases
  legislation, 12
  practice in commission, 81

Wigmore, John H., on applicability of rules of evidence to administrative tribunal hearings, 3

Wilson, district judge, quoted, 27

Wisconsin
  judicial decisions, *see* Table of Cases
  legislation, 10

Wyoming
  legislation, 9–10
  practice in commission, 81–82